The Embodied Subject

Psychological Issues
Series Editor: Morris N. Eagle

Psychological Issues is a monograph series that was begun by G. S. Klein in the 1950s. The first manuscript was published in 1959. The editors since Klein's death have been Herbert Schlesinger, Stuart Hauser, and currently, Morris Eagle.

The mission of Psychological Issues is to publish intellectually challenging and significant manuscripts that are of interest to the psychoanalytic community as well as psychologists, psychiatrists, social workers, students, and interested lay people. Since its inception, a large number of distinguished authors have published their work under the imprimatur of Psychological Issues. These authors include, among many others, Erik Erikson, Merton Gill, Robert Holt, Philip Holzman, David Rapaport, and Benjamin Rubinstein. Psychological Issues is fortunate in having an equally distinguished Editorial Board consisting of leaders in their field.

Other Books in the Series

The Embodied Subject

Minding the Body
in Psychoanalysis

Edited by
John P. Muller and Jane G. Tillman

JASON ARONSON
Lanham • Boulder • New York • Toronto • Plymouth, UK

Published in the United States of America
by Jason Aronson
An imprint of Rowman & Littlefield Publishers, Inc.

A wholly owned subsidiary of
The Rowman & Littlefield Publishing Group, Inc.
4501 Forbes Boulevard, Suite 200, Lanham, Maryland 20706
www.rowmanlittlefield.com

Estover Road
Plymouth PL6 7PY
United Kingdom

British Library Cataloguing in Publication Information Available

Library of Congress Cataloging-in-Publication Data

The embodied subject : minding the body in psychoanalysis / edited by John P. Muller
and Jane G. Tillman.
    p. ; cm. — (Psychological issues)
  Includes bibliographical references.
  ISBN-13: 978-0-7657-0527-3 (cloth : alk. paper)
  ISBN-10: 0-7657-0527-3 (cloth : alk. paper)
  ISBN-13: 978-0-7657-0528-0 (pbk. : alk. paper)
  ISBN-10: 0-7657-0528-1 (pbk. : alk. paper)
  1. Psychoanalysis. 2. Mind and body. I. Muller, John P., 1940– II. Tillman, Jane G.,
1961– III. Series: Psychological issues (unnumbered)
  [DNLM: 1. Psychoanalytic Theory. 2. Body Image. 3. Psychoanalytic Therapy—
methods. 4. Self Concept. W1 PS572 2007 / WM 420 E527 2007]

RC506.E453 2007
616.89'17—dc22   2006102125

Printed in the United States of America

♾™ The paper used in this publication meets the minimum requirements of American
National Standard for Information Sciences—Permanence of Paper for Printed Library
Materials, ANSI/NISO Z39.48-1992.

Contents

Introduction

John P. Muller, Ph.D.

The topic for this volume served as the theme of a year-long seminar conducted by the Forum on Psychiatry and the Humanities, affiliated with the Washington School of Psychiatry. The authors attempt to provide both a broad theoretical base for considering the notion of embodiment in psychoanalysis as well as some specific clinical interventions that, we could say, serve to "embody" the conceptualizations. No single point of view governs the range of ideas and observations, but I have one (Muller 2000) and will try to state it here as clearly as I can.

When we say that a sign represents an object, we mean that a sign stands for the object in a particular way, that it "embodies" or instantiates the object—not the object in its totality, but with regard to some aspect of the object. The index "you," for example, represents the addressee, in this instance **you**, the reader, not in your totality but with respect to your position in this modified dialogal relationship. When I say "you," the word marks the position and embodies the instance of the one to whom I am speaking. The word "you" is able to do this partly because it is differentiated from "I," the instance and place of the speaker, the other pole of the dialogue. The meaning of "you" is evinced in the gestures of attentive listening to the speaker. In the semiotic terms of Charles Sanders Peirce (1992), the sign "you" generates the interpretant, the meaning of the sign, insofar as the addressee attends to the speaker. The interpretant can be said to embody the meaning of the sign, to instantiate the sign's meaning, to be the particular instance of the sign's meaning. In this way, speech is both embodied (in sound and gesture) and also produces embodiment (the feelings and actions of the listener). My basic premise is that only a speaking being can be embodied, in contrast to views of embodiment in which a mind is "in" a brain or a brain is in a body, as if embodiment is equivalent to physical containment.

Physical structures, even when mingled, always remain contiguously and externally adjacent to one another. What can be embodied is what is precisely not just a body but also a sign. The embodied "mind," therefore, is no more located in the brain than it is in the voice or the hands or the gait of a person, all of which constitutes the person as a "sign" for others.

To be merely a sign for others, however, is one way to define a psychotic condition: When one is so objectified, reduced to being merely the bearer of meanings imposed or projected by family members, a relation of exteriority is established in which an individual is unable to achieve the sort of semiotic development that is required for the emergence of a subjective psychic interiority bounded and held by language. In this case, as Lacan puts it, "the subject, one might say, is spoken instead of speaking" (2004, 68). Language performs a "containing" function through the intersubjective medium of speech. When mutual recognition through speech is refused, an individual remains in an objectified state in which psychic development remains poorly differentiated, with bits of experience as "débris . . . floating in a space so vast that its confines, temporal as well as spatial, are without definition" (Bion 1977, 12; see Muller 2005).

For Bion, the elements of "raw" experience ("beta-elements") are normally transformed by a semiotic code into aspects of subjective experience that can be thought, whereas for Lacan the symbolic register marks out differences in experience that enables objects to be differentiated and desired. In other words, we humans live in a structured semiotic space that, in holding us, both constrains our grandiosity and affords us a limited range in which to generate our own meaning.

A semiotic space is one in which semiosis takes place. Peirce explicates this notion of semiosis as the triadic action of objects, their signs, and their interpretants, where interpretants are the set of signifying effects that constitute the sign's meaning, bringing new knowledge of the object insofar as new sign activity is generated by the interpretants. Peirce would like to avoid the term "interpreter," since it implies that one is in control of one's interpretations of signs in conscious mentation, whereas in actuality the interpretant effects of signs operate largely unconsciously and enable one to become an interpreter. Such effects include feelings and enactments, as well as the conceptualized meaning induced by a sign. Since for Peirce all thought operates through signs, there is no mind without semiosis. Semiotic breakdown, therefore, is equivalent to mental fragmentation and loss of a cohesive self. Patients will often attempt to forestall such fragmentation by cutting themselves, as if making a desperate effort to mark the external boundary of the skin in the absence of reliable internal semiotic differentiation.

Self-mutilation, in my view, becomes a desperate attempt to identify oneself when the usual processes of mutual recognition and identification have failed to develop. In the absence of such self-apprehension, semiotic derailment occurs, leading to an impairment in the use of signs, especially one's own affective states as signs. Hence Van de Vijver writes: "The capacity for *recognizing* the sign-function clearly requires the capacity for including one's own (organic) being in a self-referential, that is, identificatory, closing judgment" (2000, 9). The notion of "closure" here does not mean a closed system, but rather a recursive, self-referential living organization, with capacities for self-production and self-maintenance required to provide a stable internal context from which to interpret one's surroundings. She goes on to state: "A sign can only be recognized as such when someone has succeeded in making a self-referential judgment by which he takes a sign as something that stands for himself or herself in some respect or capacity. This, according to me, is the proper way in which *embodiment* should be interpreted" (2000, 9). Damasio emphasizes that "the key to the self is the representation of the continuity of the organism," and that "a likely support for the representation of organismic continuity is the neural system responsible for the representation of our own bodies" (2003, 254).

The representation of the body is a vast topic (see for example, Feher, 1989), and the histories of ideology and art have as much claim to it as does psychology. Insofar as psychoanalysis, however, is most fundamentally a theory of representation (Green 2004; Rizzuto 2001) as well as a practice of interpreting representations so they can have their proper place, then the clinical data of psychoanalytic treatment have special bearing on the issue of embodiment.

The following authors emphasize how bodily configurations and mentation are interrelated. This was noted by Freud when he wrote: "It is my opinion, however, that when a hysteric creates a somatic expression for an emotionally coloured idea by symbolization, this depends less than one would imagine on personal or voluntary factors. In taking a verbal expression literally and in feeling the 'stab in the heart' or the 'slap in the face' after some slighting remark as a real event, the hysteric is not taking liberties with words, but is simply reviving once more the sensations to which the verbal expression owes its justification" (Freud 1895/1955, 180–81).

The hysteric, Freud seems to be saying, is someone whose bodily states function as interpretants of verbal signs and who requires someone else to read these bodily states as signs in their own terms. To the extent that through our bodies we are signs to an other, signs we cannot fully perceive by ourselves, we are all hysterics. Freud's contribution, in part, was to open up this semiotic space so that a patient's symptoms could "join in the conversation" (p. 296). The following essays invite the reader to join in our conversation.

REFERENCES

Bion, W. (1977). Attention and Interpretation. In *Seven Servants*. New York: Jason Aronson. (Original work published 1970)

Damasio, A. (2003). Feelings of emotion and the self. In Eds. J. LeDoux, J. Debiec, and H. Moss, *The Self: From Soul to Brain,* Vol. 1001 (pp. 253–61). New York: Annals of the New York Academy of Sciences.

Feher, M. (Ed.). (1989). *Fragments for a History of the Human Body,* Parts 1, 2, 3. New York: Zone.

Freud, S. (1955). Studies on Hysteria. In J. Strachey, ed. and trans., *The Standard Edition of the Complete Psychological Works of Sigmund Freud,* Vol. 2. London: Hogarth Press. (Original work published 1895)

Green, A. (2004). Thirdness and psychoanalytic concepts. *The Psychoanalytic Quarterly,* 73(1): 99–135.

Lacan, J. (2004). The function and field of speech and language in psychoanalysis. In *Ecrits: A Selection* (pp. 31–106). Tr. B. Fink. New York: Norton. (Original work published 1966)

Muller, J. (1996). *Beyond the Psychoanalytic Dyad: Developmental Semiotics in Freud, Peirce, and Lacan*. New York: Routledge.

———. (2000). Hierarchical models in semiotics and psychoanalysis. In *Peirce, Semiotics, and Psychoanalysis* (pp. 49–67). J. Muller and J. Brent, eds. Baltimore, MD: The Johns Hopkins University Press.

———. (2005). Approaches to the semiotics of thought and feeling in Bion's work. *Canadian Journal of Psychoanalysis,* 13:31–56.

Peirce, C. S. (1992). *The Essential Peirce: Selected Philosophical Writings, Vol. I (1867–1893).* N. Houser and C. Kloesel, eds. Bloomington: Indiana University Press.

Rizzuto, A. (2001). Metaphors of a bodily mind. *Journal of the American Psychoanalytic Association,* 49(2): 535–68.

Van de Vijver, G. (2000). Identification and psychic closure: A dynamic structuralist approach of the psyche. In J. Chandler and G. Van de Vijver, eds., *Closure: Emergent Organizations and their Dynamics,* Vol. 901 (pp. 1–12). New York: Annals of the New York Academy of Sciences.

Chapter One

The Body in Psychoanalysis and the Origin of Fantasy

Arnold H. Modell, M.D.

It should not be news to psychotherapists that our bodies determine how we think. But how our bodies manage to do this is another matter. In this chapter, I look more closely at the relationship between fantasy and the body. Freud cemented this connection when he understood fantasy to be derived from instincts, describing fantasy as an instinctual derivative, a representation of instinct (Freud 1915/1957). We are now in a better position to understand this relation between fantasy and the body as a result of recent developments in cognitive linguistics and neurobiology. I suggest that an unconscious metaphoric process interprets bodily sensations and is a major determinant in the construction of fantasies.

The term *fantasy*, in everyday language, may refer to transitory, wishful daydreams that form part of the stream of consciousness, but that is not the kind of fantasy that I discuss here. The exemplary fantasies that I describe are not transitory, but instead form a nearly permanent part of the mind. Such fantasies could be described as self-defining fantasies, and in the examples that I give, can accurately be called malignant.

As early as 1899 Freud was aware of the importance of fantasies and their relation to bodily symptoms (Masson 1985). He observed that bodily manifestations such as vomiting and blushing could be explained as the effect of a fantasy. In a letter to Fliess (February 19, 1899) Freud writes: "you know, for instance why X.Y. suffers from hysterical vomiting? Because she fancies that she is pregnant, because she so insatiable that she cannot put up without having a baby by her last fantasy lover as well. But she must vomit too, because in that case she will be starved and emaciated, and will soon lose her beauty and can no longer be attractive to anyone. Thus the sense of the symptom is a contradictory pair of wish fulfillments" (Masson 1985, 345). Freud recognized the

1

now familiar observation that a symptom contains both the wish and its prohibition. Moreover, he observed that a fantasy can be used in the service of
self-punishment. Freud goes on to write: "You know why our friend E. turns
red and sweats as soon as he sees one of a particular category of acquain-
tances, especially at the theater? He is ashamed. No doubt; but of what? Of a
fantasy in which he figures as the de-flowerer of every person he meets. He
sweats as he de-flowers, he works very hard at it." Parenthetically, Freud does
not specify here whether these fantasies are conscious or unconscious. In an
earlier letter to Fliess (September 21, 1897), the famous letter in which he
states: "I no longer believe in my neurotica," thereby abandoning his seduction theory of the neurosis, Freud observed that there is no indication of reality in the unconscious so that one cannot distinguish truths from fiction, or
memory from fantasy. In this same letter, in which Freud wrote that it was the
fantasy of a sexual encounter rather than its actuality that was the etiological
factor in the production of neurosis, he notes that "in order for a fantasy to become pathogenic it must be reinforced by subsequent experience" (p. 264). I
return to this point later. Freud here was not opposing fantasy to reality, that
is to say, life experiences, but assumed a more complex relationship. I prefer
this earlier view, as Freud later contrasted fantasy and reality: With the introduction of the reality principle one species of thought-activity was split off; it
was kept free from reality testing and remained subject to the pleasure principle alone. This activity is "phantasying" (Freud 1911/1958, 222). He also
writes: "The strangest characteristic of unconscious processes is due to their
entire disregard of reality testing: they equate reality of thought with external
reality, and wishes with their fulfillment" (p. 225).

When in 1897 Freud abandoned the seduction theory in favor of the pathogenic influence of fantasy as an explanation of neurosis (Masson 1985), he
did not yet consider fantasy to be an instinctual derivative, for the simple reason that instinct theory was yet to be formulated. When Freud described fantasy as an instinctual derivative or a representation (for an excellent discussion of Freud's conception fantasy see Laplanche and Pontalis 1968), Freud
was confronted with the mind-body problem, a problem that contemporary
philosophy and neuroscience have yet to solve. If fantasy is a derivative of instinct, how does matter become imagination? Freud used a very clever
metaphor to account for this mysterious leap from body to mind, the
metaphor of *representation* in order to account for the derivation of a fantasy
from sexual instinct. The term *representation* is itself a political metaphor. A
(Freudian) *representation* can be thought of as a delegation, as if from one
foreign embassy to another, an ambassador from the domain of the body,
which, to be understood, must speak a language recognizable to the country
of the mind.

Let me turn now to Melanie Klein's (1948) view of what she designated as *phantasy* (in contrast to fantasy). As an observer of children, Klein knew that children live in the world of their imagination. The fact that fantasy pervades the life of children led her to the formulation that unconscious fantasy is the prime mover of psychic life; for a Kleinian analyst, unconscious phantasy underlies all mental life. In a classic paper Susan Isaacs, herself a Kleinian, states that "there is no impulse, there is no instinctual urge or response which is not experienced as unconscious fantasy" (Isaacs 1948, 70). In early childhood particular erotic zones are cathected and become the focus of unconscious phantasy. I believe that both Freudian and Kleinian analysts would agree with her observation that "the earliest fantasies spring from bodily impulses and are interwoven with bodily sensations and affects" (p. 73). In this paper she provides a clinical example that beautifully illustrates the early use of a perceptual metaphor. "A little girl of one year and eight months, with poor speech development, saw a shoe of her mother's from which the sole had become loose and was flopping about. The child was horrified and screamed with terror. For about a week she would shrink away and scream if she saw her mother wearing any shoes at all, and for some time could only tolerate her mother's wearing a pair of brightly colored house shoes. The particular offending pair was not worn for several months. The child gradually forgot about the terror, and let her mother wear any sort of shoes. At two years 11 months, however (15 months later), she said suddenly to her mother in a frightened voice: 'Where are Mommy's broken shoes?' Her mother hastily said, fearing another screaming attack, that she had sent them away, and the child then commented: 'They might have eaten me right up'" (p. 84). The flapping shoe was seen by the child as a threatening mouth and responded to as such. What Isaacs describes as the child's fantasy can also be thought of as a displacement of a perceptual metaphor that has its origins in the child's bodily experiences and is then projected outwards. This example illustrates how metaphor underlies this animistic belief—her mother's shoe became a living object that would swallow her up. It is also evident that the body is the original source of metaphor, which is then projected outwards into the world.

That the body is a source of metaphor has been amply demonstrated by the recently established discipline of cognitive linguistics. Cognitive linguistics, an interdisciplinary union of linguists, cognitive scientists, and philosophers, has shown that metaphor is primarily a form of cognition and not, as was conventionally believed, a trope, a decoration, a figure of speech. Although language is literally unthinkable without metaphor, it seems to me (Modell 2003) probable that metaphor evolved before the acquisition of language and is developmentally antecedent to language, as Susan Isaacs' example demonstrates. For centuries linguists have accepted Aristotle's definition of metaphor as a figure of speech that departs from literal meaning. The field of cognitive linguistics has conclusively demonstrated that metaphor is considerably more than a part of speech. Metaphor is primarily a form of cognition and thought, which secondarily becomes incorporated into language. As psychoanalysts we know that gestures, visual images, feelings and bodily sensations can all function as metaphors without any connection to language. These manifestations have been customarily referred to as preverbal, but that term is misleading, as gestures, visual images and bodily sensations may or may not be combined with language and can be more accurately described as para-verbal rather than preverbal.

I would define metaphor, not as an analogy as Aristotle believed, but as *a mapping or transfer of meaning between dissimilar domains (from a source domain to a target domain).* Metaphor not only *transfers* meaning between different domains but metaphor, by means of novel recombinations, can *transform* meaning and generate new perceptions. Imagination could not exist without this recombinatory metaphoric process. Metaphors are embodied in that they are generated from bodily feelings and sensations, and for this reason it is possible to speak of a corporeal imagination. The linguist George Lakoff and the philosopher Mark Johnson describe such embodied metaphors as primary (see Johnson 1987; Lakoff 1987; and Lakoff and Johnson 1999). One such metaphor is the body as a container. Johnson (1987, 21) states, "We are immediately aware of our bodies as three-dimensional containers into which we put certain things (food, water, air) and out which other things emerge (wastes, air, blood etc.)."

This pervasive kinesthetic experience of our body in space provides a containment schema consisting of a boundary distinguishing an interior from an exterior, and contents within the container. We take for granted the primary metaphor that our body is a container into which we place "good" substances and from which we expel noxious substances. From this primitive and universal experience, we form the schema that we take into the container what is good and eject what is bad. As our sense of self is originally a bodily self, we *are* this container, and the "good" that we take in becomes part of ourselves and is then unconsciously mapped onto our feelings of self-worth. What is good we identify with ourselves and what is bad as something outside ourselves, which is the, nonself, the Other. In this primitive evaluation, the non-me is bad!

Some years ago, in the paper "Having the Right to a Life" (Modell 1965) I observed an elemental fantasy that having something good for oneself takes something good away from other family members. Those who are influenced by this belief will suffer from a pervasive sense of unconscious guilt. Over the years I have repeatedly encountered this fantasy in some of my patients, so that I feel fairly confident of my original observations. The contribution of cognitive linguistics in identifying "the body-as-a-container" as a primary metaphor, has rounded out my understanding of this fantasy. The primary metaphor of the body-as-a-container leads to the following image: *when something "good" is taken into the body/self it is "all gone" and not available to other members of the family.* The transformative and generative power of metaphor is such that it can expand this primary metaphor into an organizing schema with innumerable variations. For example, the "good" that is taken into the body may be equated with mother's milk, being loved, or possessing some notable talent or high intelligence. Or, the good that is incorporated into the self may refer to one's more fortunate fate as compared to the fate of other family members. If one has a more benign fate as compared to other members of the family, this may be experienced as the result of taking some "good" away from them. In accordance with the body-as-a-container metaphor the "good" is a concrete substance analogous to food. What is "good" is ingested or in some fashion incorporated into the body/self and therefore taken away and not available to others. The individual who possesses this "good" consequently feels guilty because he or she has taken it away from others in the family. Having something "good" within one's self may lead to a kind of survivor guilt if one's good fortune is compared to the current fate of other family members and the balance of "good" is in one's favor. This unconscious fantasy may then lead to the belief that one does not have a right to a life. If one does not have a right to a life, one must constantly justify one's existence.

Possessing something good may also lead to the thought that taking away what is "good" damages the others by depriving them of something vital. If other family members, parents or siblings, are in fact damaged by illness or other misfortunes of fate, our subject's guilt will be that much increased. Some individuals have the fantasy that in the process of becoming an autonomous person, their mother was damaged. Again, this can be understood as a variation on the basic schema that the "good" is the content of a container. In order to become a separate person one takes away a "good" substance from the mother, depriving the mother of her internal matter and consequently depleting the mother and damaging her. This can be described as a form of separation guilt. A female patient, for example, was convinced that her mother's illness was caused by her emigration to a foreign country. She was convinced that the separation had in fact damaged her mother. Had she remained at home mother would not be ill. Metaphors can be dangerous when they become real.

If one believes that the "good" that one possesses has been obtained at the expense of other family members, one may irrationally feel responsible for the misfortune of others, as if misfortune is a sign that one has taken away the "good" from other family members. In another example, an unmarried woman who grew up in a family experiencing both a death of a sibling and a father's deteriorating illness felt that she could not have anything for herself. This guilt interfered with her relationships with men, for if she became aware of the man's pain and suffering, she then could not make any claims or demands for herself; as a consequence she avoided intimate relationships. In addition, she felt that she could not protect herself. In order to protect oneself one must believe in the right to do so, that is, one must believe that one has a right to have something for oneself.

What I have attempted to illustrate in these examples is that the primary metaphor of the body as a container is at the root of a fantasy that results in a pervasive unconscious guilt. One can point to such a fantasy as a biological source of a primitive morality. Such fantasies can have a decisive influence on the course of one's life.

I will now turn to another embedded fantasy that also has its origin in bodily sensations. This is the fantasy that one's love is destructive. In this fantasy, love's destructive influence includes both self and object: the destruction can move in either direction. Love may destroy the other, or one may be destroyed by the other's love. The fantasy that I wish to focus upon includes the belief that passion itself, notably the sensation of the heat of passion, is intrinsically damaging. This theme has been celebrated in myth and is familiar to opera lovers in the mythic love-death of Tristan and Isolde, who are destroyed by their passion.

An embedded fantasy that compels one to believe one's love is dangerous and can have tragic consequences for one's life conduct. An individual under the sway of such a fantasy will of necessity mount a pervasive defense against intimacy. We know that the fantasy that love is destructive was observed by Fairbairn (1952) to be an organizing belief in the so-called schizoid personality, which is withdrawn, isolated and aloof. This fantasy has also been frequently observed in schizophrenia and in borderline states.

In order to understand the relation of this fantasy to the body we must turn again to the role of metaphor and the schema of the body-as-a-container. I believe that the interpretation of bodily sensations is a highly individualistic process, so that there are many possible variations all leading to the same outcome. What I shall describe is only one possible variant. A container has contents, and feelings are universally experienced as if they were concrete substances within that closed container. Our language is replete with metaphors describing feelings as concrete substances. For example, one is *bursting* with desire; if angry, one may be about to *blow one's top*. The heightened intensity of an affective experience is then felt as a pressure within the container. Intense feelings, whether rage or sexual desire, may be felt as a hot pressure within the body seeking escape. The pressure of the feeling would threaten the container itself with disruption and disintegration. A patient who believes that to love is dangerous because of the pressure of feelings feels as if her love is a damned up reservoir—if the floodgates were opened, she would lose control and her very self would fracture and disintegrate.

Some readers may wonder: If there are nearly universal bodily metaphors, how does one account for individual differences in the formation of fantasies? The malignant fantasy that love is destructive is fortunately by no means universal. As I noted, this fantasy is most frequently observed in schizoid, borderline and schizophrenic individuals. Although anyone may entertain fleeting thoughts that one's love is destructive, happily for most of us, this is not an embedded belief determining the course of our lives. So we must look elsewhere for additional factors that might explain the determinants of this particular fantasy.

What I offer here is not a definitive answer, but merely some clues that may ultimately lead to an answer. First, let us start with the assumption that the presence of a cognitive deficit will affect the interpretation of bodily sensations. In attempting to reconstruct the origin of this fantasy, I am suggesting that there is, in some individuals, a cognitive deficit that degrades metaphor. We know that open or generative metaphors require the play of similarity and difference, and this play of similarity and difference may be lost as a result of a cognitive impairment. Degradation of metaphor is usually referred to as concrete ideation, or somewhat inaccurately as a loss of symbolic function. Such degradation of metaphor has been observed in individuals who have been seriously traumatized, in the brain damaged, as well as in schizophrenia. Hanna Segal gave the following account of a schizophrenic patient in a mental hospital: "He was once asked by his doctor why it was that since his illness he had stopped playing the violin? He replied with some violence: 'Why? Do you expect me to masturbate in public?'" (Segal 1957, 391). I will suggest that something analogous occurs with regard to the metaphorization of feeling, and that this type of cognitive impairment is not limited to schizophrenia. A degraded metaphor may take the following form: intense passion is felt as heat, heat is associated with fire and fire is destructive. With the degradation of metaphor there is a loss of the quality "as if." Let us imagine that with the loss of the "as if" quality of metaphor, an intense feeling is experienced as "hot" and this intense heat is felt as destructive.

Another clue to the origin of such malignant fantasies can be found in the observation that patients who fear that their love is destructive also experience a heightened sensitivity to all feelings. This heightened sensitivity may reflect what psychoanalysis has recognized as a disorder of affect regulation.

From this perspective a malignant fantasy is overdetermined in that internal and environmental systems are acting in concert. We hypothesize that there is the presence of both a cognitive deficit that degrades metaphor and a disorder of affect regulation. Individuals who experience a problem regarding affect regulation frequently also experience an inability to differentiate feelings, to distinguish intense rage from intense passion. We know from infant observation that the regulation of feeling is not a process that occurs within the infant alone, but that the affect systems of infant and the mother are conjoined. Although the infant has his/her own homeostatic regulatory system, the dyadic relationship with the mother or other caretakers supervenes. The infant relies on the mother's more complex consciousness to differentiate and regulate feelings. This can be expressed by Bion's famous formulation of the container and contained. It is reasonable to suppose that in the early development of someone who is destined to become schizoid and believes that love is destructive, there has occurred a developmental disturbance regarding the containment of affects.

There are other reasons besides psychopathology to believe that each of us interprets our bodily sensations and feelings in our own distinctive way. In thinking about this issue, I have found it useful to return to the traditional faculty psychology that distinguished between sensation and perception. There is some experimental evidence from neurobiology that justifies differentiating sensation from perception. The neurobiologist Walter Freeman (1995, 1999) has investigated the neurophysiology of olfaction in rabbits. He has demonstrated that when rabbits sniff odors, there is a transitory response from the olfactory receptors that can be called a sensation. This transitory response differs from a more lasting subsequent response that interprets that sensation, the more lasting response can be described as perception. Freeman investigated the electro-neurophysiology of olfaction in rabbits by means of an array of 64 electrodes attached to the rabbit's olfactory bulb. He observed that during the stage of sensation, consisting of the excitation of the receptor cells in the nose, there is no extraction of information or meaning. In fact there is no permanent record of this excitation; once having occurred, it is wiped clean. Perception occurs "behind" the receptor cells, for it is there that the olfactory bulb and the brain construct memory and meaning. Freeman observed that each rabbit constructed meaning in its own particular way, that the electrical recordings of olfactory responses could be recognized as individual signatures. One might say that perception interprets sensation to create meaning. Perception is the organization of sensations.

Without minimizing the differences between rabbits and people, I believe that Freeman has uncovered a fundamental principle regarding perception, namely, that perception is the end result of a highly individualized selective process. The reader may however raise another objection—that the perceptual inputs from the external world are not equivalent to the perception of feelings and sensations from the interior of the body. This was not Freud's understanding, however. Freud proposed an idea that is fully consistent with contemporary neurobiology: consciousness is Janus-faced, consciousness has two perceptual surfaces, receiving impressions from both the external world and the body's interior. Furthermore, Freud believed that the sensations received from the unconscious inner world, that are interpreted as feelings, are processed in a similar manner as those sensations received from the external world.

The idea of a "raw" sensation that requires interpretation in order to create meaning is reminiscent of Charles Sanders Peirce's concept of *firstness* as presented by John Muller (2000). "A feeling is a state of mind having its own living qualities independent of any other state of mind" (Muller 2000, 150). Peirce's proposal that feelings are immediately present without reference to anything else (a quality for which he created the neologism "firstness") is a good definition of a "raw" sensation. As Muller commented, Peirce's notion is that feelings are immediately present and are experienced as a form of "coerced mirroring" that leads to action. Peirce thus implied that the interpretation of a feeling can be forced and involuntary. Firstness is equivalent to a raw sensation before it is provided with context. It docs not matter whether the sensation comes from within the body or from a sensory portal. This example supports the idea that each of us interprets bodily sensations in our own way. Individual differences do matter.

As a thought experiment, let us imagine someone dominated by the fantasy that one's love is destructive. Let us further imagine that this unfortunate individual suffers both from a cognitive deficit that renders metaphors as something concrete, as well as a relative incapacity to modulate and regulate feelings. Returning to the metaphor of the body-as-a-container and feelings as concrete substances within the container, let us think of our subject, a male, as overwhelmed with erotic passion. He experiences such passion as a hot burning substance within him, and by means of perceptual metaphors associates this with fire and its destructive effects. As the body is equated with the self, the self is then seen as destructive, and contact with the object of his desire may result in the other's obliteration.

I shall now attempt to compare this hypothesis of the origin of fantasy to that of Freud. Freud described the bodily origin of fantasy, but he could not fully accept the idea of a more autonomous, idiosyncratic imagination, as that would not be consonant with the assumption of universal instincts. My reading of Freud suggests that there is a dissociation or split between Freud the scientist and Freud the humanist and clinician that creates an irresolvable tension. Perhaps the fact that he did not attempt to reconcile this dissociation is a sign of Freud's genius. In case histories and clinical examples, fantasies are recognized as creations of the individual, but not so in theory. In keeping with the scientific outlook of the nineteenth century, Freud sought to establish universal theories. I view his instinct theory as one such attempt. From this point of view, fantasy was not seen as autonomous but as a derivative of a specific (partial) instinct. It is of some interest that Freud never quite connected fantasy to the term *imagination*. I believe that Freud avoided the term imagination as it implies the autonomy of the self. If fantasy is understood to be a derivative of instincts, and if instincts are universal, Freud implied that there is a linear, causal or deterministic explanation for the origin of fantasy. In contrast, I view the origin of fantasy as indeterminate and unpredictable.

Within our gender we all inhabit bodies that are more or less similar, but this does not mean that our bodies generate uniform fantasies, as Freud implied. Fantasies are a form of corporeal imagination, and bodily sensations and feelings are subject to transformation through highly individualized memory and metaphor. We generate fantasies that are unique to us.

Freud's libido theory could be understood as a description of corporeal fantasies derived from the privileged zones of mouth, anus, and genitals which Freud interpreted in the context of universal partial instincts. Freud observed the *transfer of equivalent meaning* that results from the sensations aroused by different bodily openings such as lips, vagina, and anus. This led to Freud describing the transfer of meaning between *baby, feces, and penis*. Although Freud did not identify what he called equivalent meanings as metaphor, that is essentially what he described. In his paper "On transformation of instinct as exemplified in anal eroticism" (1917/1958, 128) Freud writes: "Feces, penis and baby are all three solid bodies; they all three, by forcible entry or expulsion stimulate a membranous passage, i.e. the rectum and the vagina, the latter being as it were 'taken on lease' from the rectum." He also states, "*But it is interesting to note that after so many détours an organic correspondence reappears in the psychial sphere as an unconscious identity*" (p. 133; italics mine). This "unconscious identity" we can now interpret as a metaphoric identity based on the interpretation of similar sensations. It is universal conviction among children, who long retain the cloaca theory, that babies are born from the bowel like a piece of feces: defecation is the model of the active birth. But the penis has its forerunner in the column of feces which fills and stimulates the mucous membranes of the bowel. When a child, unwillingly enough, comes to realize that there are human creatures who do not possess a penis, that organ appears to him as something detachable from the body and becomes unmistakably analogous to the excrement, which was the first piece of bodily material that had to be renounced. A great part of anal eroticism is thus carried over into a cathexis of the penis. But the interest in that part of the body has, in addition to its anal-erotic root, an oral one which is perhaps more powerful still: for when sucking has come to an end, the penis also becomes heir to the mother's nipple. If one is not aware of these profound connections, it is impossible to find one's way about in the fantasies of human beings, influenced as they are by the unconscious. Feces—money—gifts—baby—penises are treated (in the unconscious) as though they mean the same thing (Freud 1933/1958, 101).

I do not question the accuracy of Freud's description of these fantasies. What I do question is the implication that such fantasies are universal rather than the result of an unconscious, variable and highly selective individualized process that is indeterminate, and unpredictable. Freud's libido theory is not a reflection of universal instinct, but instead an individualized metaphoric interpretation of bodily sensations.

In addition to the problem of the origin of embodied fantasies, we also need to consider a related problem—why are these particular malignant fantasies so persistent and so difficult to modify? My experience has been that these fantasies have become so much a part of the conscious and unconscious milieu of the self that they are almost impossible to eradicate. I have repeatedly experienced that when I interpret these fantasies, to enable aspects of the unconscious to become conscious, this has absolutely no therapeutic effect whatsoever. Freud, who was by no means a therapeutic optimist, did believe in the power of making the unconscious conscious. He placed, in my opinion, an undeserved value upon the corrective influence of rational thought. In accordance with his famous aphorism, "Where id is ego shall be," he believed that unconscious fantasy could be dispelled or at least modified by means of interpretation. Unfortunately, with regard to the specimen fantasies I have described, this is not true. Furthermore, I have learned that it does not matter whether such embedded fantasies are initially conscious or unconscious; in any case they are resistant to our best therapeutic efforts. Their persistence reflects a "will to believe."

Nonlinear dynamic systems theory contains some useful metaphors that can be applied to the intractable belief systems that these fantasies create. Systems that are in steady states, systems that are resistant to change, are referred to as *basins of attraction.* The basin of attraction describes a stable state based on the analogy of a ball rolling to the bottom of a bowl. No matter where on the perimeter of the bowl it was originally dropped, the ball will come to rest at the same place. The steady state that the ball achieves after it rolls to the bottom is a confluence of a multiplicity of determinants derived from the convergence of several diverse systems. The fantasy that one's love is destructive or that one does not have a right to a life can be described as a *malignant basin of attraction*. No matter where one starts, one extracts the same meaning from experience.

The fact that an embedded fantasy functions like a template that filters the meaning of experience suggests an analogy between such a fantasy and a traumatic memory. Some traumatic memories are not recontextualized as a result of subsequent experience as is the case with a malignant fantasy. We have a ready-made concept that describes the effect of subsequent experience upon memory which could also be applied to the effect of subsequent experience on fantasy. This is Freud's concept of *nachträglichkeit. Nachträglichkeit* is better known amongst European analysts. We have not given this concept the attention that it deserves; this may be due to Strachey's misleading translation of the term as deferred action. *Nachträglichkeit* can be better understood as a retrospective attribution, a process that recontextualizes memory. Freud's theory of memory as a recontextualization first appears in a letter to Fliess dated December 6, 1896:

> As you know I am working on the assumption that our psychic mechanism has come into being by process of stratification: the material present in the form of memory traces being subjected from time to time to a rearrangement in accordance with fresh circumstances—to a retranscription. Thus what is essentially new about my theory is the thesis that memory is present not once but several times over, that it is laid down in various kinds of indications. I should like to emphasize the fact that the successive registrations represent the psychic achievement of successive epochs of life. At the boundary between two such epochs a translation of the psychic material must take place. I explain the peculiarities of the psychoneurosis by supposing that this translation has not taken place in the case of some material, which has certain consequences. (Masson 1985, 207)

The key concept here is that psychopathology results from a failure of recontextualization, or a failure of translation. The implication is that the pathological effect of a traumatic memory may, in certain cases, be minimized if that memory is recontextualized through fresh and novel experience. If, however, reality replicates or mirrors the memory of the original trauma, the pathological effect will be reinforced. Similarly, if reality coincides with fantasy that fantasy will be reinforced. The reader may recall Freud's statement noted at the beginning of this chapter, that "in order for a fantasy to become pathogenic it must be reinforced by subsequent experience." Fantasies that have become malignant basins of attraction are those that have been reinforced by subsequent experience. When external reality coincides with an autonomous, self-created fantasy, that fantasy may become fixed and indelible.

The role of reality can be seen in the observation that those who believe that they do not have a right to a life, do in actuality enjoy a better fate than that of other family members. Those individuals who are dominated by this fantasy are selected by fate to be the survivors within their particular family. They in fact do have more than other family members who may have died or become damaged through illness. Individuals may feel the need to justify their existence not only because they are alive and well, but because they do in fact have more talent, more intelligence, or other valuable attributes as compared to their family members.

The fantasy that one's love is destructive may be reinforced by the death of a parent during childhood, which the child interprets as the result of their malignant power. This fantasy may also be present without reality supervening. Not everyone who believes that his or her love is destructive has experienced the loss of a parent through death or illness in childhood. But if such a loss did occur, it will serve to reinforce the fantasy. If in addition to the child's belief in the omnipotence of thought, such an individual suffers from a disturbance in affect regulation, the intensity of the heat of feeling may be interpreted by the child as a cause of death. In any case, the real state of affairs, both internally and externally, colludes with fantasy to form a stable mental structure. Fantasy is not innate in a genetic sense, but innate in that fantasies are generated from within. Fantasies originate in bodily sensations that are interpreted selectively, but in some cases when a fantasy functions as a malignant basin of attraction, it will have been reinforced by subsequent experience.

Regardless of the origin of a fantasy, if a fantasy becomes incorporated into the value system of the self it may become intractable. We know that our experience of self is paradoxical. From one perspective, our sense of ourselves is ever changing. We have many selves; one's experience of self is not a unitary stable thing as our self-awareness is continually modified intersubjectively. From an ecological perspective, the self is continually modified by its environment, which is the other. Our sense of self will vary in accordance with the response *of* the other person to us, and our sense of self is modified in accordance with our response *to* the other person. From another perspective, one can observe a completely opposite state of affairs. What is of the utmost importance to us, analogous to the body's maintenance of homeostasis, is the maintenance of an unchanging, coherent, and continuous sense of self. From an evolutionary perspective I have suggested elsewhere (Modell 2003) that the psychological self is continuous with a biological self that originally was a monitor of homeostasis. The self perpetuates a constant internal psychological milieu that is analogous to a physiological steady state. We know that passionately held beliefs contribute to the continuity and coherence of the sense of self. It is for this reason that some individuals are willing to die for what they believe, as witnessed by the terrible events of September 11, 2001. What I am suggesting is that in addition to the reasons I have presented earlier, the persistent hold that malignant fantasies can have on the individual, can be further explained by the fact that the fantasy has become analogous to a passionately held belief, a belief that has become part of the essential nature of the self. The fantasy becomes part of one's internal environment.

In contrast, however, to passionately held religious or political beliefs that lead to action, malignant fantasies, as observed in our patients, usually produce inaction, an inhibition of action. If an individual believes that possessing something good means that one has taken away something good from other family members, that person will be unable to act in accordance with one's own self interests. In order to have something for oneself one must first justify one's existence, one's right to a life. Similarly, if one believes that one's love is destructive, one will be unable to express love and affection and will do everything in one's power to avoid intimacy.

Such fantasies cannot be abandoned because the integrity of the self depends upon their preservation. Conventional psychoanalytic wisdom has maintained that the power of a fantasy to influence behavior resides in the fact that the fantasy is unconscious. I am suggesting something different: the power of a fantasy to influence behavior results from the fact that such fantasies have become woven into the fabric of the self.

REFERENCES

Castoriadis, C. (1997). *World in Fragments*. D. Curtis, ed. and trans. Stanford, CA: Stanford University Press.

Fairbairn, W. R. D. (1952). *Psychoanalytic Studies of the Personality*. London: Tavistock Publications.

Freeman, W. J. (1995). *Societies of Brains*. Hillsdale, NJ: Lawrence Erlbaum.

———. (1999). *How Brains Make up their Minds*. London: Weidenfeld & Nicholson.

Freud, S. (1957). The unconscious. In J. Strachey, ed. and trans., *The Standard Edition of the Complete Psychological Works of Sigmund Freud*, Vol. 14. London: Hogarth Press. (Original Work published 1915)

———. (1958a). Formulations on the two principles of mental functioning. In J. Strachey, ed. and trans., *The Standard Edition of the Complete Psychological Works of Sigmund Freud*, Vol. 12 (pp. 213–26). London: Hogarth Press. (Original work published 1911)

———. (1958b). On transformations of instinct as exemplified in anal erotism. In J. Strachey, ed. and trans., *The Standard Edition of the Complete Psychological Works* of *Sigmund Freud,* Vol. 17 (pp. 125–34). London: Hogarth Press. (Original work published 1917)

———. (1958c). New introductory lectures. In J. Strachey, ed. and trans., *The Standard Edition of the Complete Psychological Works of Sigmund Freud,* Vol. 22 (pp. 1–182). London: Hogarth Press. (Original work published 1933)

Isaacs, S. (1948). The nature and function of fantasy. *International Journal of Psychoanalysis,* 29, 73–97.

Johnson, M. (1987). *The Body in the Mind.* Chicago: University of Chicago Press.

Klein, M. (1948). *Contributions to Psychoanalysis.* London: Hogarth Press.

Lakoff, G. (1987). *Women, Fire, and Dangerous Things.* Chicago: University of Chicago Press.

Lakoff, G. and Johnson, M. (1999). *Philosophy in the Flesh.* New York: Basic Books.

Laplanche, J. and Pontalis, J. B. (1968). Fantasy and the origins of sexuality. *International Journal of Psychoanalysis,* 49, 1–18.

Masson, J. M. (1985). *The Complete Letters of Sigmund Freud to Wilhelm Fliess.* Cambridge, MA: Harvard University Press.

Modell, A. (1965). On having the right to a life: An aspect of the super-ego's development. *International Journal of Psychoanalysis,* 46, 323–31.

———. (2003). *Imagination and the Meaningful Brain.* Cambridge, MA: MIT Press.

Muller, J. (2000). Hierarchical models in semiotics and psychoanalysis. In J. Muller and J. Brent, eds., *Peirce, Semiotics, and Psychoanalysis* (pp. 49–67). Baltimore, MD: The Johns Hopkins University Press.

Peirce, C. S. (1891). The architecture of theories. In *Charles S. Peirce: Selected Writings.* P. P. Wiener, ed. New York: Dover Publications.

Segal, H. (1957). Notes on symbol formation. *International Journal of Psychoanalysis,* 38, 39–45.

Chapter Two

That Subtle Knot: The Body and Metaphor

Richard B. Simpson, M.D.

As our blood labours to beget
Spirits, as like souls as it can;
Because such fingers need to knit
That subtle knot, which makes us man;

So pure lovers' souls descend
To affections, and to faculties,
Which sense may reach and apprehend,
Else a great prince in prison lies.

To our bodies turn we then, that so
Weak men on love reveal'd may look;
Love's mysteries in souls do grow,
But yet the body is his book.

And if some lover, such as we,
Have heard this dialogue of one,
Let him still mark us, he shall see
Small change when we're to bodies gone.
(John Donne, "The Ecstasy")

INTRODUCTION

In this chapter, I argue that no notion of "metaphor" can be detached from language and that, in fact, language is a key to the power of metaphor and to the way the mind functions in its conscious and unconscious forms. My appeal to John Donne is to help demonstrate that there is no getting away from language, and that a notion of cognitive functioning "apart" from language is at best an attempt to avoid the fact of language, the predominance of which has been a predominant feature of twentieth century thought. For psychoanalysts who ultimately deal with people only by the grace of words heard and said, it is important to take account of that ocean of language on which we float, even if so much of the time we take it for granted.

The Ecstasy by John Donne (1896, 53–56), one of the "metaphysical poets," gives us many metaphors and much to ponder about the body, the spirit (mind) and the soul: it opens this chapter as a counterpoint to cognitive linguistics' (Lakoff and Johnson 1999) attempt to tear metaphor from its roots in language. My claim is that metaphor is knotted inseparably with language and that its creative power comes from this knotting. Just as Donne tells us that in order to be human "our blood" must labor to beget spirits (mind) as much like souls as we can, so we listen to patients who must labor to hear that "soul" which speaks behind the words. I will return to the poem later in the chapter to discuss how Donne prophetically indicates that meaning (spirit-mind) arises in a knotting of soul (unconscious desire) imbued by love with erotic energy that must use the body to arrive at language—"But yet the body is his [love's] book."

This chapter originated from a discussion of a presentation by Arnold Modell (2003) in which he embraced Lakoff and Johnson's "cognitive linguistics" and their use of the word "metaphor," making it into a cognitive concept about the process of mapping in one direction between cognitive domains where the authors claim that this process functions "apart" from language (Modell, 2003). Lakoff and Johnson put forward their work as empirical evidence of unconscious cognitive activity, but hasten to add that this has nothing to do with the Freudian unconscious.

COGNITIVE LINGUISTICS, THOUGHT, LANGUAGE AND METAPHOR

Lakoff and Johnson write: "Each of these neural modeling studies constitutes an existence proof" (1999, 38). My reading of their empirical work is that it simply involves computer simulations of neural sensory-motor pathways that are compared in different ways with the structure of conceptual language. The process they describe appears to be more like a mathematical concept from set theory. "Existence proof" appears to mean that something can happen, not that it does happen in a human being, or how important it is if it happens. Computer simulations are one form of empirical knowledge for which face validity can only extend to computers: to make hypotheses about humans based on such "proof" is less grounded in human behavior than John Donne's lived experience passed down to us and preserved by generations for four hundred years.

Lakoff and Johnson's attempt to take the word "metaphor" and use it to name an empirical cognitive concept is troubling on a number of levels. Since the dictionary is a set of rules in human culture for how language is used, I would note that the definition of "metaphor" from the *New Shorter Oxford English Dictionary* (1993, 1756) is (1) a figure of speech in which a name or descriptive word or phrase is transferred to an object or action different from, but analogous to, that to which it is literally applicable; and (2) a thing considered as representative of some other (usually abstract) thing; a symbol.

Lakoff and Johnson have tried not only to create a neologism by using "metaphor" to name a process of mapping in one direction between cognitive domains, but also to negate the present dictionary meaning of "metaphor" as a part of language. The assertion that the referent which the word "metaphor" denotes is now supposed to be outside of language does great violence to the very process of conceptualization itself, which is embodied in language.

And as Merleau-Ponty notes, thought, which now seems to be called cognitive process, and language are in a complex relation to each other: "One could say about language in its relations with thought what one says of the life of the body in its relations with consciousness. Just as one could not place the body on the first level, just as one could not subordinate it or draw it out of its autonomy, . . . One can say only that language makes thought, as much as it is made by thought. Thought inhabits language and language is its body. This mediation of the objective and the subjective, of the interior and the exterior—what philosophy seeks to do—we can find in language if we succeed in getting close enough to it" (Merleau-Ponty 1974, 102).

Cognitive linguistics does not succeed in "getting close enough to it" because its attempt to generalize the way people use language is at odds with our experience of human subjectivity. As Kristeva notes in her book *Language the Unknown,* language in the abstract must be differentiated from human speech or discourse: "Psychoanalysis renders impossible the habit commonly accepted today by current linguistics of considering language outside its *realization* in *discourse,* that is, forgetting that language does not exist outside *the discourse of the subject* . . . The subject and meaning are . . . produced in the *discursive work* (Freud spoke of the dreamwork) . . . The production of meaning is . . . an actual production that traverses the surface of the uttered discourse, and that engenders in the *enunciation*—a new stratum opened up in the analysis of language—a particular meaning with a particular subject" (Kristeva 1989, 274–75).

The difference between language in the abstract versus the discourse of the subject echoes the distinction between the systemic level of the semiotic, involving the recognition of signs, and the semantic level, requiring the understanding of the meaning of words actually used (Benveniste 1974; Agamben 1993).

A corollary of this view of discourse is Lacan's most general definition of interpretation, to the effect that one is always saying more than one knows one is saying. In "The Agency of the Letter" he specifies: "What this structure of the signifying chain discloses is the possibility I have, precisely in so far as I have this language in common with other subjects, that is to say, in so far as it exists as language, to use it in order to signify *something quite other* than what it says" (Lacan 1977, 155).

In the clinical vignette to follow, one could say that I was informing my patient that he was saying more about the word "edge" than he knew he was saying.

CLINICAL VIGNETTE

The following clinical material is presented to give an example of a way of looking not only at the content of the patient's speech, but also at the very way words are used by the particular person speaking. One way of conceptualizing this aspect of speech is with Saussure's (1966) concept of "linguistic value" which will be defined later but, suffice it to say here, includes metaphor and all the contextualized properties of speech in actual discourse.

The patient was a man in his thirties in twice per week psychotherapy for several months. He had intermittent symptoms of bulimia, and in his early life he had been exposed to a father who was distant, non-supportive and at times sexually provocative. His mother was the more stable figure for him but she managed her life by using massive amounts of denial and keeping busy. He was experiencing depressive symptoms—feeling empty, lack of motivation and feeling he could not see a future for himself. He felt he needed antidepressants and asked for them. My sense was that he had an accommodating character structure and tried to construct himself according to the demands of the environment at the expense of being able to articulate his own desire. It was a time in the treatment process when he appeared to be trying to change his behavior with his family and within the transference.

I agreed to his request and he started the medication which I thought might help him pharmacologically but, more to the point, I saw his request as a test of how I would respond to him. He was asking for a response from the environment and I took his request for medication as a sign of his desire to have the pain he was suffering acknowledged. Thinking in terms of semiotics, one might say that prescribing medication was my gesture to him, an index of my having registered his suffering and so an acknowledgment of its existence. Such an acknowledgment could perhaps assist him to develop a representation of his own suffering as his own.

After two weeks on the medication he said he was not doing much better. At that same point, he said maybe it was not all about the antidepressant. He said that he would like something "to take the edge off of it." I can't recall exactly how I put it, but I said something like "perhaps his having an edge" was part of what was troubling for him. I spoke of a shirt that he mentioned in the previous session, a shirt he had worn that his family did not see fitting their way of dressing and so he had risked their rejection. He had worn the same shirt in another part of his life where a different sense of fashion could also have disapproved of him. I said that his wearing the same shirt in both places indicated he was trying to maintain something of himself in both locations rather than dressing in each environment in a way that would blend in with the people around him at the time. The implication was that the shirt was an "edge," in the sense of a border, defining him as separate from the environment.

In the subsequent session, he felt better. He said he had started to say to himself, "Just stand inside yourself." At the same time, he felt a change of his perception of material reality around him. In "standing inside himself" he realized that he had previously experienced himself as "out there," rather than within his own body. He went on later to say that this idea of having an edge had struck him, although he has not been directly aware of it, because he had previously felt himself to be "like water on a table that runs according to gravity."

I would like to focus on how the patient's word "edge" was used for its linguistic value (Saussure 1966, 110). Linguistic value is a term from Saussure's theory of the linguistic sign that I find very useful since it refers to a property of language that is not specifically about meaning. What I said to the patient made a shift from the use of "edge" in the English idiom "to take the edge off," meaning "to get relief from" to the use of "edge" indicating a border, a limit; here "edge" specifically referred to the patient's mental experience of his body. I was taking "edge" out of the idiom in which he used it and moving it to a more fundamental signification defined as "border." What allows this shift to happen is the linguistic value of the word "edge." Linguistic value means all of the possible ways "edge" can be used in English, that is: (1) the sounds of the letters, the phonemes [e –de- g]; (2) all of the meanings of the word itself; and (3) all the combinations with other words, including idioms that yield significations different from the primary definitions of "edge."

I recall feeling unsettled about taking his word "edge" and turning it in another direction. It was partly doubt about my clinical assessment but it was also the unsettling feeling of walking on the thin ice of language. It seems solid enough if you tread softly but when you jump up and down on it, you worry about breaking through into the depths of unformed, unnameable chaotic experience.

Clinically this patient had difficulty putting his experience into words. At times of stress with other people, he would binge and vomit in a manner that gave him some relief from a psychic state he could not put into thought. Binge eating and vomiting were interpreted later to him as possibly indicating an action on his part at the level of his body where something was put inside and then put outside. This very action of a movement from outside to inside and back to outside marks the border of inside and outside, as we do when we underline something on a page. The area that he was marking on the page of his body, the mouth and lips, was the border of that erogenous zone Freud called oral. He was able eventually to describe an experience of confusion between the inside and outside by noting that after he could say to himself "stand inside yourself" he could then retroactively put into words that his previous un-thought state was that of seeing himself as "out there." One might say that the patient was able to use words ("stand inside yourself" and "out there") in order to experience the boundary of his body as secure rather than marking this boundary by taking in food and vomiting it out in order to secure the boundary. What is most important for us in this clinical material is that an inchoate experience of the patient concerning subject-object differentiation came into his speech, his discourse. I took note of how he used words, rather than my putting words into his mouth.

LANGUAGE AND SYMBOLIC CAPACITY

At the level of clinical thinking where patients have difficulty being able to put inchoate experience into words, there have been many different approaches to the same territory that Modell explores (chapter 1 of this volume) when he uses Lakoff and Johnson's cognitive linguistic term "metaphor" to try to name this phenomenon. Modell cites Castoriadis' phrase the "corporeal imagination," which Castoriadis himself describes here: "Kant is thinking of a body that is an automaton for producing blind sensations. But this is not true. The body creates its sensations. Therefore there is a *corporeal imagination,* which, in the human being, goes hand in hand with a new dimension of the radical imagination properly speaking, the emergence of this incessant flux that is at once representational, intentional and affective. Through the two of them are created a "proper world" of the human subject, which is no longer the proper world of the animal; it is not given once and for all . . ." (Castoriadis 1997, 178).

We can note here that Castoriadis says the body "creates" its sensations and the "proper world" of the human subject is not given once and for all. This would indicate that the corporeal imagination is not a cognitive neurological structure, but is involved in a vital interchange with the *radical imaginary*. Later in the same volume, Castoriadis makes it clear that his vision of the radical imaginary is profoundly social, comes from human-life-as-a-collective and creates language: "Language [is] the creation of the radical imaginary, that is to say, of society. Language as such and singular languages are, each time, a creation of the corresponding collectivity" (p. 185).

Thus even Castoriadis' vision of the corporeal imagination exists only in a relation to language as the material manifestation of the human collectivity that Castoriadis calls the radical imaginary.

Hans Loewald (2000, 439) wrote his final treatise on "sublimation," his way of conceptualizing higher orders of complexity in psychic development. And Lacan, in his own way, was always addressing the complexity of human signification, ultimately in the knotting of the three registers of experience: the imaginary, the symbolic and the real. In this same territory, I have thought of patients in terms of *symbolic capacity*. Symbolic capacity refers to the way language can work for people to allow the creation of levels of complexity and the movement of meaning in the direction of the psychic elaboration of inchoate experience that is in the borderland between mind and body. For indeed Freud's (1915/1957) invention of the concept of the "drive" was exactly "a concept on the frontier between the mental and the somatic," and he defined the drive as "the psychical representatives of the stimuli originating from within the organism and reaching the mind, as a measure of the demand made upon the mind for work in consequence of its connection with the body" (p. 120). Leclaire, in the opposition of "organic" and "psychic" terms, underscores: "The difficult concept of the drive, which constitutes Freud's true contribution, tends to comprehend precisely this dualism within a truly novel dynamism. The originality of this concept described as a limit, is that it grounds the unconscious outside the categories of the biological and the psychological understood in their pre-Freudian sense. In other words, the division or gap grounding the dimension of representation in the whole doctrine of the drives is without question situated elsewhere and otherwise than in the traditional opposition between the soul and the body" (Leclaire 1968, 40).

Rather than jettisoning the drives from theory as passé, it seems clear that the concept of the drive is Freud's tool for thinking that gives us the very ground between soul and body where symbolic capacity needs to grow.

There is another feature of metaphor that refers to the question of symbolic capacity but which escapes its dictionary definition. As Northrop Fry (1990, 72) notes, "Metaphor with the 'is' predicate says explicitly 'A is B' (e.g. 'Joseph is a fruitful bough,' Genesis 49; 22), and conveys implicitly the sense 'A is quite obviously not B, and nobody but a fool would imagine that Joseph

really was,," a fruitful bough. The more stunning the opposition of the "is" and
the "is not," the more powerful the metaphor can be in its capacity to alter
how we see things. Andrew Bowie (2003, 45) notes in reference to the early
philosopher of language Hamann that "Language is essentially *creative*, and
it is inseparable from the capacity to reveal new aspects of existence which
we often associate with art. In consequence, attempts to fix an order of things
in language fail to appreciate language's 'Dionysian' aspect, which allows it
constantly to refashion the ways in which the world is revealed to us." When
John Donne in *The Ecstasy* declares "And yet the body is his book" the body
as "his [love's] book" is more than a figure of speech, it is the creation of an
identity between the idea of a book and the idea of the body. And as a creation, it still has the power, after four hundred years, to make us wonder.
Wonderment comes exactly because it is an identity that defies the confines
of identity.

And indeed in the light of psychoanalysis, we can read "the body is his
[love's] book" to indicate that the body is the location of traces left by the
erotic touch of an other (usually the mother) whose desire leaves its mark.
Serge Leclaire has written of this erotic body being marked by areas of ten-
sion/release in the model of Freud's pleasure principle where these areas of
"pure difference" (Leclaire 1968, 47), a kind of inchoate ripple of differentiation, can be thought of as creating letters. Whether one follows Leclaire in
his extension of Lacan's notion of the letter or not, the so-called letter or trace
that is conceptualized here is at a distance from what presents itself in consciousness as the presentation. As Laurence Kahn (2001) has pointed out,
what is presented to consciousness in dreams or slips is not the representation
(*Vorstellung*) but the presentation (*Darstellung*).

The act of becoming conscious by means of a presentation is not at all
similar to the formation of a presentation or idea by which consciousness
lays down before the mind that which is its object of thought (Freud 1900/
1953). We have, therefore, to take into account the difference in the use of
the terms *Vorstellung* and *Darstellung* that is maintained in a perfectly dis-
criminating manner in Freud's work. The ideational and referential contents
of "representation" and "presentation" are kept separate, to the extent that
the latter is capable of being unlinked seemingly from any system of reference (Freud 1900).

This capacity of the "presentation" of perceptual elements in a dream, a
symptom or a way of saying something to be unlinked from seemingly any
system of reference makes finding the representation of the trace or letter subject to absolutely individual variations. It is in this area between the presentation of perceptions and the representation of the trace or letter that symbolic
capacity plays a role. Furthermore, there is the question of how one conceptu-

alizes the trace or letter. In a footnote, Leclaire links the notion of letters marked on the body with Derrida's idea of *"différance"* and he quotes Derrida:

> It is not a question of a constituted difference here, but rather, before all determination of content, of the *pure* movement that produces difference. *The (pure) trace is différance.* It does not depend on any sensible plenitude, audible or visible, phonic or graphic. It is, on the contrary, the condition of such a plenitude. Although it *does not exist*, although it is never a *being-present* outside of all plenitude, its possibility is by rights anterior to all that one calls sign . . . concept or operation, motor or sensory . . . . It permits the articulation of speech and writing—in the colloquial sense—as it founds the metaphysical opposition between the sensible and the intelligible, then between the signifier and the signified, expression and content, etc. (Leclaire 1968, 62–63)

Leclaire has connected here the erotogenic body of Freud's drive theory with Derrida's theory of the pure "trace" and so Leclaire speaks of the erotogenic body as the place where signification arises in conjunction with human desire, and this knotting of the letter and desire in the body constitutes precursors of language.

The important point in all of this theory is how can our work help patients develop symbolic capacity or whatever one might call it—the elaboration of fantasy, the corporeal imagination, or the process of sublimation. For certainly, it is often not the content of the fantasy that is at stake but that there can be fantasy at all rather than action or somatization. Helping patients to develop the capacity to form fantasy, to have that possibility of a mental life that binds in some manner what has gone on before and allows the person to experience a complexity of mental scenarios is clearly something we all struggle with. Alan Bass (2000) approaches the problem from the other direction, the problem of concreteness as a resistance to interpretation. He sees concreteness as a demand that something mean one thing, and only one thing. Such concreteness is a resistance to the whole process of differentiation, or one might say a resistance to the possibility of metaphor, imagination or symbolic capacity.

JOHN DONNE'S METAPSYCHOLOGY

It is from poetry that we can learn about imagination and how words can be used, as in John Donne's vision of the body as love's book. In the first part of the poem, two lovers on the bank of a river are in a wordless reverie all of a long day. Donne imagines the ecstatic (from the Greek: *ex* "out of, out" + *histanai* "to cause to stand") movement of the soul of each lover outside its body, which remains like a statue and cannot speak. Then, in that refinement which love engenders in the soul, each soul can speak but only in the language of the soul. And the language of the soul is a strange "dialogue of one" because each one speaks the same meaning and each cannot tell itself from the other. So in this ecstatic movement out of the body, the two "interanimated" souls come to be one purified soul. But being human, the body cannot be forgotten or escaped and so the "blood" of the body labors to create a spirit (mind) that will articulate between the soul and the body, and this spirit aspires to be as much like the one purified soul as possible. Being human, having a body, means one needs to knit that "subtle knot" between the soul, the spirit (mind) and the body:

> Love's mysteries in souls do grow,
> But yet the body is his book.

And in this work of creating spirit (mind), by way of the mysterious power of love within the souls, humans cannot understand the language of the soul directly but they must read from the body, which is love's "book." And so the body is the intermediary, the place across which must be born the language of the soul for the body to become readable. The *New Shorter Oxford English Dictionary* tells us that metaphor is composed from *meta,* denoting a nature of a higher order or more fundamental kind, and *pherein*, to bear. One could say that in Donne's poem what was born in the inarticulate language of the soul is transferred into a higher order of nature by means of the body. And so, the body is the location of a bearing across or transfer to a higher order, a *meta-pherein*, a literal meta-phor.

Although evidently not a cognitive linguist, Donne may be considered a meta-psychological poet. By that I mean, he created names for orders of experience, as does psychoanalysis, where the carrying of something inchoate (soul/the dialogue of one) through erotically imbued sensations on the body leads to language (spirit/mind) and to our humanity. Rather than allowing metaphor to fall captive to one-dimensional cognitivist terminology, we have much more to gain by keeping metaphor's myriad possibilities within language and realizing those possibilities in our daily psychoanalytic work.

REFERENCES

Agamben, G. (1993). *Infancy and History.* L. Heron, trans. London: Verso.

Bass, A. (2000). *Difference and Disavowal: The Trauma of Eros.* Stanford, CA: Stanford University Press.

Benveniste, E. (1974). *Problèmes de Linguistique Général, 2.* Paris: Gallimard.

Bowie, A. (2003). *Introduction to German Philosophy: From Kant to Habermas.* Cambridge: Polity Press.

Castoriadis, C. (1997). *World in Fragments.* D. Curtis, ed. and trans. Stanford, CA: Stanford University Press.

Derrida, J. (1974). *On Grammatology.* G. Spivak, trans. Baltimore, MD: The Johns Hopkins University Press.

Donne, J. (1896). *Poems of John Donne,* Vol. I. E. K. Chambers, ed. London: Lawrence & Bullen. [Complete poem available online at http://www.luminarium.org/sevenlit/donne/ecstacy.htm]

Freud, S. (1900). *The Interpretation of Dreams.* London: Penguin Freud Library.

—— (1953). The interpretation of dreams. In J. Strachey, ed. and trans., *The Standard Edition of the Complete Psychological Works of Sigmund Freud*, Vol. 4. London: Hogarth Press. (Original work published 1900)

—— (1957). Instincts and their vissicitudes. In J. Strachey, ed. and trans., *The Standard Edition of the Complete Psychological Works of Sigmund Freud,* Vol. 14 (pp. 109–40). London: Hogarth Press. (Original work published 1915)

Fry, N. (1990). *Words with Power.* New York: Viking Penguin.

Kahn, L. (2001). L'action de la forme. *Revue Française de Psychanalyse,* 65, 983–1056.

Kristeva, J. (1989). *Language the Unknown.* A. Menke, trans. New York: Columbia University Press.

Lacan, J. (1977). *Ecrits: A Selection.* A. Sheridan, trans. New York: Norton.

Lakoff, G. and Johnson, M. (1999). *Philosophy in the Flesh, the Embodied Mind and its Challenge to Western Thought.* New York: Basic Books.

Leclaire, S. (1968). *Psychoanalyzing: On the Order of the Unconscious and the Practice of the Letter.* P. Kamuf, trans. Stanford, CA: Stanford University Press.

Loewald, H. (2000). *The Essential Loewald.* Hagerstown, MD: University Publishing Group.

Merleau-Ponty, M. (1974). *Consciousness and the Acquisition of Language.* H. Silverman, trans. Evanston, IL: Northwestern University Press.

Modell, A. (2003). *Imagination and the Meaningful Brain.* Cambridge, MA: MIT Press.

New Shorter Oxford English Dictionary. (1993). Oxford: Clarendon Press.

Saussure, F. (1966). *Course in General Linguistics.* C. Bally and A. Sechehaye, eds., W. Baskin, trans. New York: McGraw-Hill.

Chapter Three

The Concept "Superego": Another Look (Up to Par or a Hole in One?)

Lila J. Kalinich, M.D.

INTRODUCTION

In a paper entitled "On the Body of Conscience" (Austen Riggs Center, Stockbridge, MA, April 23, 1993), I argued that for women, the structures of self-restraint and self-criticism are intimately linked to concerns about body integrity. Using clinical material to demonstrate my point, I also claimed that since the female experiences her body as something outside of her control, she experiences those structures and "objects" that help her to maintain control as outside of herself as well. I concluded that her "superego" reflects her sense of the unreliability of her body. Like her body, she tends to experience the superego's locus as external.

So then, I threw my hat into the ring of what feminists would call "essentialism" and Freudian essentialism at that. In other words, I concluded that the structure of a woman's superego is intimately linked, if not determined, by the structure of the genital she has. I had years earlier made a similar foray in my paper "On the Sense of Absence" (Kalinich 1993). Therein I explored the influence of genital experience on cognition and memory. In that paper, however, I made no claims about a particular psychic agency. I found no need to extend the argument to a consideration of the integrity of the "ego" as such. When it came to talking about conscience, however, I did feel constrained by the terms of the debate as it has raged since Freud made his controversial claims about the female superego.

After giving the paper, I made an initial contact about submitting for publication. But I never did. There was something about the paper that troubled me. Although I believed that the clinical points I had made were sound, I nonetheless felt that I had entered a debate about whether or not unicorns really have horns. It seemed to me that trying to say something about the structure or content of the "superego" carried with it a logical problem of serious proportion. It was rather like attempting to characterize the rules of operation of poker through a description of a deck of cards. This led me to reconsider the utility of the structural hypothesis as it has come to be applied. The recent work of Charles Brenner (1994) has emboldened me to do so more seriously.

Further, while the paper lay fallow, I returned to teaching in the undergraduate Freud course at Columbia College. There I encountered young women and men who were so politicized by the recent debates over gender roles and gender polarity that they resisted the notion that human beings are gendered at all. They had more interest in refuting Freud than in actually listening to what he had to say. It was often difficult to persuade them to take Freud in context, to measure him against the backdrop of the century from which he had emerged. Instead they were inclined to treat him as a misguided contemporary thinker, as merely a misogynist rather than the liberator of women that he actually was.

Yet many of these students, so strident in their criticism of Freud, sought personal consultation from their instructors for a panoply of pathology—eating disorders, depression, self-mutilation, suicidality, impulsivity, poor object choice (affairs with professors, passing homosexual liaisons), etc. Even though anti-Freudian, they wanted help. It seems to me that these young people have closed the door on Freud because the profession has failed them. Like Freud with Dora, we have failed to listen carefully enough. We took Freud too literally as a theoretician and too lightly as a clinician. We entered into a politically correct discourse intended to rescue women from Freud's critical gaze. Instead of grasping that Freud's insights about female development were in many ways accurate even though *incomplete*, we argued that Freud was wrong about women. We took umbrage at his paternalistic and denigrating tone at the same time that we embraced the very theory that led him to his conclusions. It is my impression that as a result, we have underestimated the psychological hazards of female development, we have relegated a generation of young women to superficial care, and we have pushed psychoanalytic theory to places it need not have gone. Rather than arguing for the wholeness of the "superego" in women, perhaps psychoanalysis and women would have been better served by looking for the "hole" in the concept "superego."

BEFORE AND AFTER THE STRUCTURAL HYPOTHESIS: FREUDIAN THEORIES OF FEMALE DEVELOPMENT

Early in his career Freud maintained the belief that psychic development of girls and boys followed essentially the same trajectory. As Strachey notes in his introduction to Freud's paper "Some Psychical Consequences of the Anatomical Distinction Between the Sexes," written in 1925, Freud wrote no significant case material about a woman patient for about fifteen years after the Dora case (Freud 1961c, 245). Although Strachey believed that the germ of the new thesis appears in Freud's earlier work, it is clear that during that long hiatus, Freud evolved a different view. During that same stretch of time Freud was also reworking his model of the mind, moving away from the topographic theory toward what was to come to be known as the structural theory. "The Ego and the Id," Freud's last theoretical paper, which articulates the relationship of the three psychic structures, "ego," "id," and "superego," was written in 1923. So it is actually *after* the postulation of the structural hypothesis that Freud gives full expression to the impact of the genital difference on the castration complex and penis envy, the dissolution of the Oedipus complex, pre-Oedipal and Oedipal object relations, and of what we will call for the sake of discussion, structures of conscience.

In 1924, in "The Dissolution of the Oedipus Complex," Freud writes that since fear of castration is not available to the girl as a motive to establish the "superego," such a motive must be an external one: "In her, far more than in the boy, these changes seem to be the result of upbringing and of intimidation from the outside which threatens her with a loss of love . . . Renunciation of the penis is not tolerated by the girl without some attempt at compensation. She slips—along the line of a symbolic equation, one might say—from the penis to a baby. Her Oedipus complex culminates in a desire, which is long retained, to receive a baby from her father as a gift—to bear him a child. One has the impression that the Oedipus complex is then gradually given up because this wish is never fulfilled"(Freud 1924/1961b, 178–79).

By 1925 Freud makes an even stronger claim. In "Some Psychical Consequences of the Anatomical Distinction Between the Sexes," describing "penis envy" and its effects, Freud declares that in boys the Oedipus complex is "smashed to pieces by the shock of threatened castration" (Freud 1925/1961c, 257) with the superego as its heir, while in girls, the Oedipus complex is slowly abandoned. And then Freud writes, "I cannot evade the notion (though I hesitate to give it expression) that for women the level of what is ethically normal is different from what it is in men. Their superego is never so inexorable, so impersonal, so independent of its emotional origins as we require it to be in men. Character traits which critics of every epoch have brought up against women—that they show less sense of justice than men, that they are less ready to submit to the great exigencies of life, that they are more often influenced in their judgments by feelings of affection or hostility—all these would be amply accounted for by the modification in the formation of their superego which we have inferred above" (p. 58).

Six years later, in "Female Sexuality"(1931/1961e), Freud emphasizes the girl's long-lived and passionate attachment to the mother. This attachment is eventually transferred to the father after the hostility toward the mother, which emanates from the girl's castration complex, sets in. The girl's hostility toward the mother is not taken to be the consequence of her Oedipal rivalry. Rather, it is simply reinforced by pre-Oedipal oral sadistic desires and frustrated infantile masturbation. (Where all of these early drives went to in the male child is yet another matter!)

By 1933 Freud makes his final statement on female psychology. In "On Femininity," he says about the superego of women that it cannot attain the "strength and independence which give it its cultural significance" (Freud 1933/1964a, 129). Later in the same lecture he says: "The fact that women must be regarded as having little sense of justice is no doubt related to the predominance of envy in their mental life; for the demand for justice is a modification of envy and lays down the condition subject to which one can put envy aside" (p. 132).

It seems that in Freud's transition from the topographic theory to the structural, he also shifted from an intricate dynamic description of the conscious and unconscious developmental factors that create obstacles to full sexual and ethical maturation in the female, to proclamations about her ultimate structural inadequacy. Freud did not draw the lines of demarcation among the structures rigidly. In fact to do so was contrary to the very complexity of the systemic interaction he was trying to articulate. Therefore a weakness in one structure necessarily demands an extension of the weakness to other parts of the system. A "weak superego" therefore implies a more general mental inadequacy if the structural hypothesis is taken seriously.

It was against this final devastating judgment that Freudian critics, particularly early psychoanalytic feminists, reacted. They staunchly opposed the notion that women suffered an irredeemably weak defective mental structure because of their genital reality. Besides, a weak mental structure sounded too much like a displacement upward from a denigrated view of female anatomy. The conclusion demanded by this version of "essentialism" was unacceptable. Further, any premise that dictated a radical irreversibility in a psychological manifestation of an individual's subjective ontology seemed contrary to the entire spirit of psychoanalysis.

It is of interest that the demise of Freudianism is contemporaneous with the ascendancy of feminism. I am not suggesting that a negative reaction to Freud and to his final theory entirely accounts for the prominent role that feminist thinking has in our culture. This would be to minimize the arduous work of the political feminists who fought for suffrage and for equality for women in the workplace. I am however saying that the tone and content of the reactive valorization of women that has ensued, and from which all of our young people suffer, is in a measure a rejoinder to Freud and to the power of the culture of psychoanalysis. As the reader has no doubt heard, women are better, nicer, kinder, and smarter than men. By the 1970s there were "studies" that provided "evidence" that women routinely had multiple orgasms during intercourse while men, of course, could have only one. We "learned" that the orgasms women achieved through masturbation were more "intense" than those during intercourse (Hite 1976). So much for Freud's view that any female would perceive the male genital to be a "a superior counterpart to her own" (Freud 1925/1961c, 252). *Au contraire!* Masculinity became a "problematic." Men were encouraged to find their "feminine sides." Homosexuality, no longer considered a diagnosis or a deviation, in its own way became valorized. With today's opportunities for alternative modes of conception, women don't need men at all! The death of desire between the sexes is really not an issue. Should desire arise, male impotence, now increasingly prevalent, can be managed with Viagra purchased without a prescription from a Web site.

Women analysts did grapple with the Freudian problem. There were those of course who, proving Freud correct about the longevity of the paternal transference, simply and lovingly capitulated to Freud. They did so brilliantly, and made serious contributions to analysis in their own right (e.g., Deutsch 1944). Others split with Freud and made dogged efforts to come up with alternative hypotheses. Horney (1950) and her followers rightly emphasized the influence of culture in gender role configurations, but the gloss seemed less and less psychoanalytic and more and more sociological or anthropological. Her work nonetheless opened the door to the rigorous feminist criticism that followed her.

FEMINIST CRITICISM

Subsequent generations of serious feminist Freud criticism have followed basically two tributaries. Each organizes itself around issues taken to transcend an individual's genital awareness or perception of the genital as such.

The first is the object relations/interpersonal stream. These two schools of thought can be grouped together, since what they share surpasses their differences. What drives these feminist perspectives is that each finds the origin of a woman's psychological difficulties in the relational world. The object relations feminists concentrate on conscious and unconscious factors, pre-Oedipal and Oedipal, which construct a woman's sense of self in the world, while the interpersonalists focus more on the cultural and political factors of the world itself. Nonetheless in each case, the woman is seen as "in relation to" rather than as a separate emerging subject. See Chodorow (1989) for full elaboration of this topic.

The object relations theorists place great emphasis on the significance of the gender of the "mothering person," arguing that primary parenting by a female yields a masculinity that is reactive, defensive, and problematic, though carrying with it the benefit of a separate sense of self (Chodorow 1989). For the interpersonalists, the masculinity problem is a cultural creation in which both men and women participate. Each gender devalues feminine affiliative qualities in favor of traditional male ones. Both groups call for a revalorization of those qualities of the feminine self—those of connectedness, empathy and nurture—over institutionalized forms of separateness such as the rigidly defined separate self, technical and scientific "objectivity," and even capitalist evaluations of the accumulation of individual wealth. Both finally demand a reformulation of the "psychoanalytic self" in which "separateness, not connectedness, needs explaining," in which the "mutual recognition" of the self and the other are taken to be central to any version of healthy development (Chodorow 1989, 185). Both emphatically reject the causal role of gender apperception in the formation of gender identity or gender personality.

The second tributary of feminist Freudian criticism is the linguistic, mainly Lacanian, view that holds that subjectivity is fundamentally gendered in that it emerges through a linguistically structured unconscious that is embedded in a network of transpersonal signification which Lacan (1978) calls the "Symbolic." In that all signifiers and symbols function with reference to other signifiers and symbols, a subject is sexed only by virtue of sexual difference. The "phallus" stands for that difference, particularly as represented by the father, whose psychological intervention as an Other, interferes with the mother-infant dyad. The immediacy of that dyad is taken to blur the distinctions necessary for the construction of subjectivity. It is this move, by which the subject is sexed, that constitutes his castration, his submission to the "Law of the Father." Language, at heart a system of differences that operates according to its own laws, is the phallus supreme. Since the phallus is not the penis, albeit a marker of the masculine in a gendered world, its possession need not be congruent with genital anatomy. The Lacanian view is generally unsympathetic to the tendency of the object relations/interpersonal group to idealize women and mothers. However, radical feminists do find it appealing to construe the phallus as a symbol that can be separated from gender identity per se. One can, in theory, "have it all."

In some respects each of these approaches seems eminently sensible to me. In fact I believe them to be indispensable to one another. Certainly the matrix of early object relations influences the reception of language. Likewise the reception of language determines how those objects and their relations come to be represented. I cannot imagine that Lacan would object to this understanding, given the importance he gave to both transgenerational histories and individual subjective development. It is deeply and fundamentally true that object relations and language acquisition are absolutely contingent upon one another. There could be nothing that object relations theorists call the "representational world" without a mind already structured by a system of differences, essentially linguistic. The object relations/interpersonal proponents take issue with the Lacanians, because phallocentrism seems inevitable among beings who become gendered in the way Lacan describes. Likewise the Lacanians criticize the object relations/interpersonal theorists for a failure to understand gender relations as a systems problem in which male and female are equally affected. They find the maternal focus inadequate to a totalizing dilemma. In turn, the object relations/interpersonal lists take Lacan to be antihumanist because they see no opportunity for social change in a Lacanian universe.

In this instance it seems to me that the "anti-Lacanians" underestimate the power and flexibility of language. Although it is governed by its own rules, the Logos remains in a condition of "Becoming." Language changes and, as a result, it changes us. Along with mind, language is an emergent phenomenon. In ancient Greece, the Athenians cut the wings off the goddess Nike to ensure that "Victory" would stay in Athens (Hornblower and Spawforth 1996, 1044). What we would call "concrete thinking" characterized all ordinary thought in classical times. Today it is considered disordered. Thinking and speaking have changed thought itself. Ideas are a penetration of life by what Lacan would call the "Symbolic"—a more powerful agent of social change than any form of social manipulation could hope to be.

In "Civilization and Its Discontents," Freud's claims about women and society are ironically quite similar to those made by the objects relations/interpersonal feminists. Recall that Freud considers affiliation, the "replacement of the power of the individual by the power of the community" as the "decisive step in civilization" (Freud 1930/1961d, 95). Further, he states that "love" opposes the interests of civilization while civilization threatens love (p. 103). Women, the very women who "laid the foundations of civilization by the claims of their love," who "represent the interests of the family and of sexual life," come to be a "retarding and restraining influence." The work of civilization, then, becomes the business of men, confronting them with ever "more difficult tasks"(p. 103). Freud seems to be saying, in contemporary-speak, that civilization *is* a "masculine problematic," not just phallocentric but the phallus itself. Clearly those political feminists who wish to undermine all hierarchical institutions from science to capitalism would completely agree. They militantly embrace a stand that is in determined opposition to the business of civilization as so construed. Where they differ is in the valuation of their stance. Freud sees the anti-progressive, or frankly regressive, quality of women as a problem. He concludes this passage by saying that civilization requires men "to carry out instinctual sublimations of which women are little capable" (p. 103). This is yet another example of the penchant for proclamations of negative judgment that characterizes Freud's work after the structural theory. Once again, Freud weakened a developmental analysis that would otherwise be interesting and useful.

Carol Gilligan's remarkable work comes out of the object relations school of feminist criticism. Examining the writings of moral theorists such as Freud, Piaget, and Kohlberg, among others, she argues persuasively that the study of the lives of real women provides a different moral conception than the one that organizes men. Unlike men, they are not governed by rules and universal principles of justice. Rather, women are grounded by issues of care and sensitivity to the needs of others. Their moral conflicts derive from conflicting personal responsibilities, complicated by a desire for approval or love. Ongoing attachment rather than individual achievement is the "path to maturity" for a woman (Gilligan 1982, 170). Gilligan sensibly claims that men and women embody two complementary moral perspectives, each representing a different but necessary dimension of human concern: the "justice perspective draws attention to problems of inequality and oppression and holds up an ideal of reciprocity and equal respect," while the "care perspective draws attention to problems of detachment and abandonment and holds up an ideal of attention and response to need. Two moral injunctions—not to treat others unfairly and not to turn away from someone in need—capture these different concerns" (Gilligan, Lyons, and Hanmer 1990, 102).

Brown and Gilligan (1992) describe the predicament of one of the preadolescent women in their lengthy study at the Laurel School in Cleveland, Ohio. The very ordinariness of the girl's difficulty demonstrates a certain point. Jessie at age eleven had already learned the virtues of "cooperation." She took standing up for herself to be "fighting." When asked about what would happen were she to "fight" with one of her friends, Jessie expressed her belief that her friend would cry and scream at her. Jessie feared she would lose her as a friend. But when pushed for more details, Jessie painted the picture of a needy friend who was unlikely to abandon Jessie under any circumstances. Jessie nonetheless let this fear of loss govern her decisions.

Gilligan uses this example among many others to show how the care perspective functions in the adolescent girl. Gilligan would never suggest that Jessie had achieved an ethical maturity. Certainly the task of unraveling her concern for her relationship from her own dependent needs remains ahead for

Jessie. It is precisely this agonizing tangle that is the ethical challenge for women young and old. And it is at this juncture that psychoanalysts who are willing to put aside the insult of Freud the theorist in favor of Freud the clinician have something to offer. Recall Freud's words: "I cannot evade the notion (though I hesitate to give it expression) that for women the level of what is ethically normal is *different* from what it is in men. *Their superego is never so inexorable, so impersonal, so independent of its emotional origins as we require it to be in men*" (Freud 1925/1961c, 257; italics mine). Gilligan has proved Freud right.

THE NATURE OF THE PROBLEM

Grounding ethical decisions in a perspective of care, complicated by anxieties about separation, is an enormous psychological problem. It is well and good to say that the difficulty is generated by those laudable feminine qualities that mitigate the harsher aspects of the male justice perspective. Women do play a vital role in keeping society human. Nonetheless, when it comes to the particular woman, this kind of conflict can be regressive and paralyzing. Furthermore, it seems to me, essentialist that I am, utter folly to propose a psychological theory that ignores what Heidegger might call the "Facticity" (Heidegger 1926/1962, 82) of the body. I say "Facticity" because I am in search of a term that carries a greater ontological reality than "fact." Lacan would call it the "Real." Gender fact, unlike gender identity, gender role, or gender personality carries the same irreversible imperative as death. All the surgery and hormones in the world will not alter its early imprint. The ego, as Freud said, is first and foremost a "bodily ego" (Freud 1923/1961a, 26). The challenge for psychoanalysts, unlike social theorists, is to relate anatomical reality (the Real of the body), to the psychic registration of social experience (what Lacan would call the Imaginary), to the unconscious generativity of language (the Symbolic).

Freud in his wisdom did link female psychology to the female soma, but did so in a way that exclusively referred to the girl's recognition of the genital contrast. He was ill-equipped to explore how having a female genital inscribed itself on the psyche of the girl. Recently several women analysts have written about aspects of what has come to be called "primary femininity" (Stoller 1976). The late Elizabeth Mayer (1995), Phyllis Tyson (1990), the late Doris Bernstein (1993), and Donna Bassin (1982), for example, have made immensely valuable contributions. In addition, infant researchers and child analysts have provided data about crucial developmental landmarks in the acquisition of primary gender experience.

My earlier work ties primary genital experience to intrapsychic representations of the body, the process of thinking, objects, and finally structures of conscience. Like Freud, I find these to be inextricably linked, affecting one another in an ongoing dialectic that just does not stand still. I place great importance on the fact that the vagina is a non-sphinctered orifice that cannot contain its contents. The experience of menstruation functions powerfully to reorganize earlier experiences of vaginal discharge or other forms of "leakage" (urethral or anal). Through what Freud calls "deferred action" or what Lacan calls the *après coup*, these trivial episodes assume the stature of traumas or threats to the girl's sense of physical and mental integrity. She maps the vaginal representation onto the "running" of her mind, ascribing to her mind an inability to contain memories, concepts, and facts. Furthermore, and perhaps of greater significance in the context of this chapter, the intrapsychic vaginal representation becomes tied to and organizes anxieties over separation. Because of the girl's representation of how the vagina functions, or fails to function, fear of object loss simultaneously threatens loss of the contents of her body. Ideas, affects, and impulses to action can, and often do, symbolize these "contents." She will then enlist external objects to help her maintain control. The paternal phallus often seems ideally suited for this task; however, any important object will do.

The question of whether the female experiences the locus of control as inside or outside seems to me to be a spurious one given the fact that we are considering psychic representations, all of which reside within the interior. In this case "superegos," for as long as I will use the term, are like belly buttons. Whether you prefer "innies" or "outies" is simply a matter of aesthetics. Each functions perfectly well.

Let me offer clinical material from a twice-weekly psychotherapy supporting this hypothesis. At the time of the session reported here, Beth was a recently married young woman with a prominent obsessional structure. Her parents had an intact but conflicted marriage that encouraged her to see herself as an Oedipal victor in some respects. She lived by a scrupulous moral code, structured around a superstitiously installed system of checks and balances. These functioned to defend her against both her greed and her incestuous desires. At the time that she started her therapy, she was not conscious of her considerable rage. She experienced it as anxiety and panic. She was very inhibited sexually. She worried that her husband would leave her because of her inhibition. The following is from our first meeting after one of my two-week vacations:

> I was away for the first week but the second week was very difficult. I got very worried about not having any sexual desire for my husband. I woke up in panic with all my questions. What have I done to him?

I am having recurrent dreams of being sexually attracted to other men. They are very erotic, but it doesn't carry over to my husband.

I had another terrible dream. I dreamt that my brother-in-law died, and I was there telling his three-year-old daughter that she'd never see her daddy again. My brother-in-law is away. All she does is ask when Daddy is coming home. I just sobbed in the dream to think of how sad it was that this little girl would never see her daddy.

I read a magazine article discussing how children interfere with a couple's relationship. This should be a time of freedom for my husband and me. And it's supposed to get worse. I worry that I will never work this out.

Although aware of all of the transferential implications of this material, I intervened on point with the topic of her immediate concern, namely, her sexual responsiveness. I interpreted from the Oedipal side, saying that at the moment her erotic life seemed invested in what she could not have.

That strikes a chilling chord. I can't believe you actually said that. It's just like my father. He's always in search of something.

Having observed that she tended to disavow all physical functions, I said here that it seemed difficult for her to allow herself to have a body, to allow sex to be about her body rather than something that is only part of a romantic fantasy. She responds in an interesting way:

I haven't smoked now for a month and a half. It's very hard. The other night my husband and I went out for dinner with friends, and after dinner, with coffee, the four of them lit up. I got so restless that I could barely sit still. We made plans to go to another place for drinks. Driving there I asked my husband whether it would be all right for me to have a cigarette. "Absolutely not!" he said. "How can you expect me to condone your smoking?" So then I said to him, "Why shouldn't I have a cigarette if I want one?" He got angry with me and got so mean. We stopped at a red light. I jumped out of the car and screamed at him that he was being so mean. I slammed the door and went home. I just had to go to sleep.

Here I pointed out how she set her husband up—that she asked his approval but no doubt also hoped he would restrain her. She agreed.

Yes, I know I did. When he returned home, I apologized. It's just so difficult not to smoke. It makes me sad . . . Yes, sad. It's a loss. Not smoking leaves a hole. Something is missing.

We finally watched our wedding tape. The most touching part was watching my parents toast one another. I thought to myself that that's the part of the tape I'll watch after they are gone. I've been thinking a lot about that lately.

"You are the little girl in the dream," I replied.

Yeah. I just sobbed and sobbed. But it's funny. My sister says she remembers that it was my mother that I always cried for when my parents would leave. I would scream inconsolably. I really am concerned that I am going to lose control of this and reveal it to my husband.

She then paused. With her eyes down she said:

And I got my period—after six and a half weeks. So it really was a hard week.

This brief moment in a lengthy treatment—would that it were a psychoanalysis—captured most of the dilemmas with which Beth was to work over the years. It nicely demonstrates how her object ties and issues of separation are intimately interwoven with concerns about her body and its competence, both as a sexual being and as a containing agent. Pre-Oedipal and Oedipal themes are inseparable from one another, just as are issues of both affective and physical control. The hole in her life created by the portent of death is symbolically represented by the hole in the body that threatens her. The body-grieving is the body-bleeding. Her body compels her to a biological destiny— motherhood—and endangers her with its desire. The easy displacement from the genital to the oral is abundantly clear. Beth enlisted the phallus to help her maintain control. Although this vignette does not demonstrate it, she used superstitions to invoke a more powerful phallic presence in the form of what Lacan would call the Law, a paternal principle that she hoped both to engage and to control.

Freud the clinician would have comprehended many of Beth's difficulties, but he probably would have glossed them in terms of "feelings of castration." The phrase works well enough if taken in a larger existential context. He would have found an externalized "superego" function, utilized to defend against condensed oral and genital drives and vaginal anxieties. His understanding would have been accurate, however incomplete. The point to be emphasized is that Freud would have been absolutely correct to tie this patient's object-related concerns to a deeply encrypted somatic apprehension that achieved its structure after menarche.

VISIBLE AND INVISIBLE

Beth's dream about the death of the father provides a clue to still another developmental hazard for women. This is again one originating in her experience and her representation of her body, and it likewise affects the shape and quality of her conscience. It revealed itself to me in a very moving way only after a recent session.

In the years that have intervened since the example above, Beth has had three children. She has a very good marriage, despite the fact that she still suffers from sexual inhibition about which she can barely speak. She is a very good mother, albeit an anxious one. A few weeks ago her son developed a life-threatening illness that might have been a reaction to a vaccination. This challenged her capacities to function more than anything ever has in her relatively sheltered life. She called upon her superstitious magic to no avail. She felt entirely overwhelmed and on the brink of a deep darkness that shook her very existence. Unable to eat or to sleep, she looked like a dry twig that the gentlest breeze could overturn. On the day of the session in question, her son still in the hospital, she collapsed into the chair; weeping, she reported the following dream:

> It's about a boy named Don. It's in a school somewhere. He is wearing a backpack. He is younger than my son. I see that he doesn't look well. I ask him if he is okay and he says, "Not really. I don't really feel well." I go off to try to find out who he belongs to and I find these two sisters who are talking and talking and are really busy. I say to them: "Can't you see that he is sick? Can't you see?! Can't you see that he has a fever?" He's burning up! (Here she weeps with grief and exasperation.) I go back to the boy and I see that he has his head down and has fallen asleep. He lifts his head and looks at me. I take his backpack off.

I encouraged her to work on the dream, believing that its illumination would find her a path out of her dark place. "Why Don?" I asked.

> He was the little brother of these two sisters who were very much a part of my life. Donna was my very best friend. I haven't been in touch for a while. We were inseparable for a long time; from about age five to age nine or ten. I wonder why I am dreaming about Donna?

"The family resembles your family (of origin). Two sisters and a little brother," I interject.

> I always said that my son reminds me of my brother. My sister and I were so mean to him. Donna was the older of the girls and her mother always preferred her sister Ellie. Her mother was a real witch. And we have been watching Snow White a lot lately. I don't know why my little one doesn't find it frightening. I find it frightening.

She returns to the topic of her son's illness, how hard it is to "see" him suffer, wondering why she "sees" no hope. Addressing the guilt in her associations,

I said: "Needless to say, you think back to all the times that you felt you were too harsh or mean to him."

She weeps. "And I am furious with Dr. Q." She described the source of her fury:

> He refused to go out on a limb, to take a stand, to do what was right for my son, because he wanted to avoid conflict. And because he is so *dispassionate*. He called me Mrs. P. And I am not Mrs. P. I am Beth. Mrs. P. isn't so bad. I can deal with that. But I told him I would prefer if he used my first name. He said, "That would be difficult for me." Well fuck him!! Too difficult for him?! How could I have trusted him? And I am furious that he gave him that shot. I told him that I didn't want him to have it. I called my sister because I was afraid he would have an allergic reaction. But I thought, "He needs it." Why did I go along with him? What made me turn against myself? How could I have not protected him? You know how superstitious I am. How could I have failed?

It was clear from this material, in both the context of the patient's lengthy treatment and her subsequent associations, that her negative transference to the boy's physician occupied both maternal and paternal loci. Dr. Q. simultaneously represented both her passive mother, unable to tolerate confrontation, and her self-involved father, whose narcissism made him indifferent to family conflicts until they impinged upon him personally. Neither parent seemed to have been effective in helping the patient to manage her aggression, especially toward her little brother, and in turn, therefore, toward her young son. Neither seemed adequately to have fulfilled the paternal or the phallic function. As a result, the patient demanded an omnipotence from herself, which she reinforced by a magical obsessional system of checks and balances. If not sheltered by the phallus, she had to *be* the phallus. She had once trusted and idealized this handsome young doctor. She believed he had offered her a sanctuary. He had allowed her the relief she found in occupying what Lacan would call the "feminine position," the condition of "lack." He seemed to have provided her with the protection of the phallus until he insisted on assuming the feminine position himself. As the patient said, "Fuck him!" Furthermore the doctor had failed, as father, to protect the child from the poisonous witch mother. Psychologically, Beth was both. This accounted for her immense guilt over her son's illness. She believed she had caused it.

Though Beth's dreams are separated by an interval of six years and vastly different life circumstances, they reveal a sustained synchronic structure. The common affect is grief and the common signifier is the word "see." Recall that in the first dream the patient's reported words were that the child would never "see" her daddy again. Later she spoke of watching and revealing. In the second she sobbed, "Can't you see, can't you see?" This dream carries with it the poignant context of her son's nearly fatal illness.

Both dreams, and certainly the latter, are reminiscent of the first dream of chapter VII of *The Interpretation of Dreams,* the dream of the burning child. Freud claims that a woman patient who had heard it at a lecture told him the dream. She then appropriated it, redreaming it. Some speculate that Freud in turn found it in his own dream life and used it to forge the path of dream theory. The dream goes like this: A father, whose sick child has just died, goes to sleep while an old man is left to keep vigil over the dead boy's body, laid out in a coffin in the next room. The father dreams that his son, standing beside his bed, tugs his arm and says with reproach, "Father, don't you see I'm burning?" (Freud 1900/1953, 509). The father awakens with a start to discover the old man asleep, the child's arm on fire from an overturned candle. Freud concludes that "I'm burning" was probably a phrase actually spoken by the febrile boy during his illness, while "don't you see" referred to past events unknown. He uses the dream to demonstrate the fulfillment of the father/dreamer's preconscious wish that his son still be alive (p. 510). In the case of my patient, her associations confirmed an analogous wish that it be someone else's child and not her son who was so afflicted.

Leonard Shengold, in his lovely book entitled *"Father, Don't You See I'm Burning?,"* relates the dream to Freud's personal history—to the death of his father when Freud was forty-one; to the death of his brother Julius when Sigmund was nineteen months; to Freud's Promethean ambition and incestuous desires. He concurs with Freud that "'Father, don't you see I'm burning' refers to repressed childhood wishes" (Shengold 1991, 51). But Shengold also links this dream to Freud's desire for recognition from his father who thought young Sigmund would "come to nothing"(p. 52). This dream then, like the two of my patient, is about what Lacan has called the "solicitation of the Gaze" (Lacan 1978, 70).

It has always been my intuition that the dream of the burning child was the dream of a woman about a dead little girl. I must make a conscious effort to correct my recollection of this dream almost every time I hear it. Perhaps this is why I was so struck when I heard Beth's version of it. Now to be seen by an Other, and to see that one is seen, and finally to see oneself seeing that one is seen, are essential steps in the development of subjectivity. The seer performs the structuring function, becoming the third term that cleaves the mother-infant dyad. This process, which creates a consciousness of oneself in relation to others, is a crucial one for both genders, but because of the complexity of the girl's path of simultaneous identification and dis-identification with the mother, "seenness" is even more invested for the female. Questions of visibility and invisibility become vitally important to her. They are of course complicated by her genital configuration, which the female can neither see nor easily show. (Remember those days not so long ago when feminists started to encourage young women to use mirrors to try to "see themselves"? This was considered a significant act of liberation.) To the extent that the genital imprint contributes to her self-concept, and I have argued strongly that it does, the female is predisposed to a sense of invisibility that is overcome only through the clear-sighted recognition of the Other.

Some have commented on how a girl's inner genital awareness contributes to a tendency to a certain feminine wiliness or secrecy. This is much different from the feeling of invisibility that I wish to emphasize here. Invisibility is a much more serious issue. A girl burns with desire for the recognition of the Other, particularly of the father. Without it, she is dead as a subject. Without it she achieves only the status of an object to be consumed by another's desire. Straightforward incestuous wishes are regularly comingled with the seduction of the Gaze. However, the desperation and the tenacity of the Oedipal demand that clinicians often encounter in female patients transcend Oedipus as such. It is more often a fight for (subjective) life.

In Lacan's commentary on the dream of the burning child, he asks, "Is not the missed reality that caused the death of the child expressed in these words? Is not the dream essentially an act of homage to the missed reality—the reality that can no longer produce itself except by repeating itself endlessly, in some never attained awakening?" (Lacan 1978, 70). Later he says "the terrible vision of the dead son taking the father by the arm designates a beyond that makes itself heard in the dream"(p. 58). It is the "beyond" that is the "nucleus" (p. 68) or "navel" or that "something primary"(p. 60). It is the place of the Real that fantasy conceals, the point around which the "syntax" of the subject's story condenses. The body unsymbolized is the body trapped in the Real. It becomes the nidus around which neurosis crystallizes. The female genital, in that place between perception and consciousness, unseen and often unnamed, excluded from symbolization, becomes the blind spot.

Somewhat paradoxically, some women take refuge in their sense of invisibility. Surely you have heard women patients express surprise that they have been remembered, recognized, or even noticed. Traditionally put, it can serve as a defense against exhibitionism and aggression.

Roberta is a young dancer who came for treatment because of her frustration over her lack of success in the last years of training at one of the nation's most prestigious ballet schools. She once had been a star at the school, but with the approach of puberty, Roberta seemed to have more difficulty capturing the attention of her teachers. For the most part she believed that her teachers passed her over for parts because of their irrational preferences for less accomplished dancers. Although she knew that she felt encumbered by her breasts, she did not really comprehend the connection between her attitudes toward her body and her problems with dance. She complained that she felt "invisible" but paradoxically refused to wear makeup. This was despite encouragement from the ballet mistress to do so. Her teachers encouraged her to "come out" more, but Roberta really did not understand what they meant. She thought she was doing everything they asked, but for reasons unclear to her, they simply did not see her. Roberta's therapy illuminated her competitiveness and exhibitionism as well as the conflicted phallic identification that covered her unseen parts. She was able to become more expansive as a dancer, and she was eventually hired by a professional company. Recently, she was not chosen for a part she felt she deserved. She described how she retreated to the back of the studio to conceal her anger, which she claimed to have quickly controlled. Later in the session she said, "I am afraid I'm becoming invisible again, just like at school. And I don't know when it started." What she meant was that she thought "invisibility" to be the *cause* of her failure to be cast, not the result of her reaction to her sense of it.

In some instances women require invisibility in order to function sexually. The lights must be out, so to speak, so that their true subjectivity remains unseen. This is the case for Beth. The source of her sexual inhibition lies in the *showing* of her desire. Speaking it is even too great a revelation for her to tolerate. A male patient of mine with a rather flexible sexual appetite established a steady relationship with a young woman who seemed to match his hunger for sexual adventure. He and others saw her as a seductive young vixen. He was excited by her interest in a *ménage à trois*, one that would add another woman to the mix. This had been a topic of conversation for several months. Recently she told my patient that she still wanted to "do it" (i.e. have sex in a threesome), but she no longer wanted to do it with him. Now that she sees him as her boyfriend and likely husband, she no longer wants him to see this side of her. Early in the relationship my patient was crazed by his suspicions of her infidelity, inflamed by her diary and emails, which he shamelessly invaded. It was as though she dared him to "see" what she was doing. She actually gave him her email password. Once he did see, once he declared himself to be the Law, she settled down and became a loving but boring sexual partner. If the Law is not blind, she will put out its eyes.

The dream of the burning child and the dreams of my patient Beth can be construed as dreams about the blindness of the Law, and in particular, the blindness of the Law to the requirements of feminine subjectivity. The failure of the father to confer subjectivity through the structure of the Gaze, or, put it another way, the failure of the girl to establish herself as a visible subject in the eyes of the father, can create an out-Law, a woman who lives as though her behavior is beyond ordinary purview. Hedda, another of my young women patients, and a very wealthy one, shoplifted on the day she was coming for her session. She claimed that she did it for amusement, that she did not feel guilty until I took the gesture seriously. This same young woman had been molested by a family friend when she was a young adolescent. She told her father at the time, but he did nothing about it. Several years later, while visiting her father, the patient found the molester in the house again. Hedda experienced her father as blind to her victimization. She took this as a startling betrayal. She felt invisible to him. Subsequently, she repeatedly and unconsciously challenged the father *as* the Law to take notice. Now she reserves her petty violations for session days. As she put it, "You make me feel guilty, but I know I make me feel guilty but you make me feel guilty if you know what I mean." This repetition seems to be helping her to acquire a "seenness" that is giving her a fuller experience of both subjectivity and conscience.

This dynamic has a social dimension as well. Insofar as women are not granted status as full subjects or citizens under the law, they take themselves to be outside of both its scope and its reach. This is especially evident among women who feel oppressed in one way or another. For them, deviance can be a way of life. Surely Freud would have called this "superego weakness," a weakness organized by the structure of the object relations or "care perspective" and grounded in the genital reality of being female. As culture changes and women do attain a more equal place, the expression of this particular female trait will change as well. But as we know from the example of former First Lady Hillary Rodham Clinton in the Oval Office, some women will nevertheless retain the capacity to use invisibility and blindness to their advantage, even when in a position of power.

I do not mean to suggest that women have a corner on the market of deviance or deceit. Men suffer serious pathologies of conscience as well. We need only to point to the example of Hillary's husband to be assured of that. However I do conclude, with Gilligan and others, that the structure of the problem and its depth are different when the source is the "measuring stick" of phallic competition.

THE HOLE IN THE THEORY

Freud devised the structural model to cope with his growing awareness of the complexity of mental life. He came to appreciate that neither consciousness nor organization were indices of rationality. The topographic model, which assigned all irrationality to the system Ucs., was inaccurate. To address this problem, he proposed three interdependent mental "structures"—the "id," "ego," and "superego"—that were supposed to work something like mathematical "mapping sets," grouping together similar functions that seemed to operate consistently over time. This model provided an immense theoretical advance in that it gave psychoanalysts a systematic way to think about the intricate lattice of psychic events. From it came an elaboration of the concept of defense, as well as the refined clinical technique of working from the surface of resistance to the depth of transference that Fenichel (1941) so elegantly described.

However Freud's desire for consistency, reinforced by the demand for it by his followers, burdened the theory unnecessarily. Recall for example the fuss that Strachey made over an interchange between Ferenczi and Freud in Appendix A following "The Ego and the Id" (Freud 1923/1961a, 60–62). Ferenczi picked up an internal contradiction in Freud's use of the terms "descriptive" and "dynamic" to describe the unconscious. Strachey struggled to rectify the difficulty, one that Freud ultimately ignored. Eventually Freud too moved away from a model that tolerated inner structural tension and toward an internally harmonious characterization of his "structures." In doing so, he simultaneously moved away from clinical observation. The next generation of psychoanalysts did so as well. We need only to think of Hartmann and the primacy of ego psychology to make the point (Hartmann 1958). Though it is true enough that the post-Hartmann years have seen substantial clinical work, it is my impression that much of that work has been forced, as well as guided, by the structural theory. I will return to this point later.

A commitment to structural theory carries a tendency to reify the structures. Although we regularly remind ourselves that we were talking about "groups of functions," our sentences treat them as real things. Boesky makes this point in his discussion of Charles Brenner's revolutionary paper "The Mind as Conflict and Compromise Formation," in which Brenner basically discards structural theory in favor of the simpler, more particular concept. While arguing on the behalf of the old theory, Boesky says that we paid a price for the use of the word "structure" because we use a "noun to connote a dynamic process" (Boesky 1994, 511). He would prefer a verb form instead but strains to find one that works. While he concedes Brenner's basic criticism of structural theory, namely, that the concepts "id," "ego," and "superego" create false separations, Boesky argues that the need to account for the stability of the very mental conflict we are trying to explain demands some notion of abiding psychic structures. Brenner's idea of "compromise formation" is, as far as Boesky is concerned, simply a psychic agency at a lower level of abstraction. Boesky's discussion reveals the conundrum clearly. But it does seem to me that the virtue of the lower level of abstraction provided by a structure called "compromise formation" tolerates more complexity, the very complexity that challenged Freud to abandon the topographic model. I believe it allows for something more like the description of the new physics that appeared in the *New York Times* "Science Times" on March 20, 2001: physics is a "story not of a clockwork world but an entangled interactive world whose constituents derive their identities and properties from one another in endless negotiation—a city, in one physicist's words, of 'querulous social inhabitants.'" This description captures a model of mind as well, an electrically quick tangle of endless negotiations. Who is to say that those negotiations would not tend to come out the same way each time—hence atomic and psychic structure? But the immediacy of a brand new negotiation creates the possibility for psychic change at any moment.

Boesky is onto something extremely important in his point about the use of nouns in the appellation of the psychic structures of the structural model. Freud himself used the Latin "ego" early in his work. The use of the term was in intellectual fashion in the psychology and philosophy of the era (Ellenberger 1970). But the *Standard Edition* translation bears most of the responsibility for the introduction of the Latin terms into common English use. One is inclined to assign culpability to Strachey, but his collaborators, Jones and Riviere, share it with him.

Das Ich, *das Es*, and *das Uberich*, the "I," the "It," and the "Above-I," became the "ego," the "id," and the "superego." The crucial grammar shifts in the translation are the moves from the indexical "I," from the pronoun "it," and from the even more interesting "anything above the indexical 'I' that refers to its user and therefore is above the user." In ordinary English, the speaker does not recognize the Latin as substitutive for pronouns as he or she does with foreign words, particularly nouns that have been thoroughly assimilated, such as *quiche*, or *coup*, or *chaise*. We never hear, for example, "'Je' was going to the store," or "I like 'id.'" We do hear lengthy philosophical discussions of the "I," as a part of speech. And we do hear versions of "My 'ego' is not strong." Now an "I" as a pronoun cannot have a problem even though its user can. I can love or hate, be weak or strong, be depressed or not, but the "I" cannot do any of those things unless I do them. The only problem that the "I" can have is to fail to refer to me when I use it, and that remains a failure of the user. So "ego," "id," and "superego" are compulsively taken for nouns. As English speakers, we have no other linguistic choice.

But something grammatically stronger is going on here. "Ego," "id," and "superego" aren't just nouns. We don't call them, as in computer-speak, "processor," "hard drive," and "monitor;" or even "thinker," "beast," and "guard," though "censor" did work pretty much in that way. These are all perfectly good nouns. The terms of the structural theory work linguistically more like the Genus, as "*Homo*" in *Homo sapiens*. These are beings with qualities, not groups of functions.

The stronger point is that we treat structure names as proper nouns. Think of how regularly "Ego," "Id," and "Superego" appear in capital letters. These Latin words are untranslatable as nouns; they refer only to themselves. So in effect they function as proper nouns or names. "Ego" implies the phrase "the structure Ego," Id, "the structure Id," and Superego, "the structure Superego." This is similar to "the man James," "the woman Nora," and "the cat Ulysses."

In his work *Naming and Necessity* Saul Kripke calls proper names "rigid designators" (Kripke 1972, 5). To state his idea of rigid designation, he asks us to consider the proposition "Aristotle was fond of dogs." He assumes that everyone can agree that there was a philosopher named Aristotle. Therefore the proposition is true if and only if Aristotle was fond of dogs. He contrasts this with an analysis by Bertrand Russell who thinks it should proceed as follows: "'The last great philosopher of antiquity was fond of dogs;' which in turn should be analyzed as 'Exactly one person was last among the great philosophers of antiquity, and any such person was fond of dogs.'" Kripke argues that someone other than Aristotle might have been the last great philosopher of antiquity and "Russell's criterion would make *that other person's* fondness for dogs the relevant issue" (p. 7).

Now my point is simply this: using names for the functional sets of the psyche leads us to talk about them as though we were discussing whether or not Aristotle was fond of dogs, perhaps even outlining the kinds of dogs Aristotle liked and the kinds he did not—such as good dogs and bad dogs. Sometimes we talk about where the dogs are located in relation to other dogs and whether or not they bite. Then we give the dogs names. And then the dogs have puppies, and so it goes. We should, in matters of theory, be doing something else. Thinking about whether or not Aristotle *was* in fact the last great philosopher of antiquity is closer to the kind of theoretical debate we need to have.

Others have complained, and like Bettelheim (1983), ranted over the years about the effect of the Strachey translation on psychoanalytic theory. Mahony says, for example, that Freud's "processive and tentative language" gives way to "closure and stasis" (Mahony 1982, 31). Furthermore using the Latin, the language of the Church no less, converted these ideas into sacred cows. Freud's use of *das Ich* and *das Es* was consistent with the intellectual discourse of his day. Had these concepts stayed within that discourse, they could have been more naturally checked against, and invigorated by, a larger community. We could call that community the *Uberich* in its truest sense. Lacan grasped the enormity of what is at stake in this Freudian notion, more deeply perhaps than Freud did himself. The "Above-I" connotes more than the Oedipal legacy understood within the family. It is, in addition, the whole of civilization, however discontented. As Kierkegaard states it in *The Concept of*

Anxiety, "If the prohibition is regarded as the awakening of desire, the punishment must also be regarded as awakening the notion of the deterrent. I have adhered to the Biblical narrative," he continues, "and have presumed the voice of punishment as coming from without" (Kierkegaard 1844/1980, 45). *"The speaker is language"* (p. 47; italics mine).

THE BARKING DOG

Let's return to the dogs for a moment. In my view the St. Bernard of current theory is the "borderline" concept. The Kris Study Group monograph by Abend, Porder, and Willick (1983) treats this topic extensively. Carefully examining case material over a four-year period from four patients who seemed to qualify for this diagnosis, the group attempted to sort out whether the borderline group of patients represented a distinct clinical entity, and undertake a serious and very respectful debate with the prevailing view of "borderline" pathology. Utilizing Kernberg as the major proponent of that view, the authors write that Kernberg himself suggested they consider pathognomic of the borderline personality organization "the presence of certain characteristic mental phenomena," *namely,* "unique defenses and distinctive forms of internalized object relationships . . . related to phase-specific developmental disturbances and prominent conflicts over aggression" with "characteristic transference behavior derived from these underlying *defects* . . . " (Abend et al. 1983, 24). The authors did so but ultimately found that their "four cases did not demonstrate constitutional abnormalities or defects." The Kris Study Group all but discards the "borderline" concept and strongly concludes that the term "does not refer to a specific diagnostic entity but to a diffuse and heterogeneous group of patients who are sicker than the more typical neurotic but not as severely disturbed as patients with psychosis . . . [They found] no specific etiological determinant of such pathology"(p. 241). "Borderline," says the group, "is at best a loose supra-classification." The study undermined the authors' belief that ego functioning was something that they understood well. Instead they found that it turned out to be "more complicated, multifaceted, multidetermined, and variable" than they had appreciated (p. 243). The Kris Study Group's final statement is about treatment: "What is of vital importance is careful analytic attention to the transference and countertransference distortions which can be so disruptive to the treatment situation, and a courageous preparedness for very slow progress. No more than the exercise of conventional analytic skills and an understanding of familiar analytic concepts is called for provided they are employed with unusual tact, patience, confidence, and persistence" (p. 243).

I do comprehend the point of nosology. Psychoanalysts need to be able to communicate with psychiatrists, and psychiatrists, with the medical and insurance worlds. When properly applied, it does help us to think in an organized way. Nosology also provides the comforting illusion that we know something even when we do not, that we are doing science because we have come up with new categories.

But too frequently it has been used in the service of discrimination. For example, psychiatric nosology in the United States is historically tied to the origin of the census. The census was a political effort to use the budding science of statistics to help cope with the growing problem of welfare. As Grob (1991) recounts, in 1888 the recognized expert on the care and treatment of dependent groups, including the mentally ill, published his *Report on the Defective, Dependent, and Delinquent Classes . . . as Returned at the Tenth Census*. In it he wrote: "There is a morphology of evil which requires to be studied. For the information of the legislatures it is important that the whole extent of the evil to be contended against be known" (Grob 1991, 424). Later he speculated about the connection between mental illness and sex, race, and national origin. This, needless to say, became fodder for enthusiasm for eugenics early in the twentieth century, as well as for the sexism that denied women the vote (p. 425) As events toward the middle of that century painfully confirmed, the belief that a group of people shares a defect has seldom come to good.

It seems to me that to claim that patients, even very sick patients, or their "egos," have a defect is at best misguided and at worst dangerous. We tend to call patients "borderline" when they are difficult to treat, when they cause us trouble, when their view of reality challenges our own. The diagnosis can be a veil for the incompetence or the inadequate training of the therapist. It can be a cover for the therapist's rage. It is not unusual for a supervisor to see a change in a patient's diagnosis as the treating therapist or analyst acquires more skill and self-understanding. The prevailing wisdom about the treatment of the "borderline" relies heavily on limit setting, always a benefit for the unruly patient. But these treatments also tend to stay organized around conscious phenomena that can give them a kind of cookbook quality. Although this is of some help to young learners, such a programmatic approach outlives its usefulness when it interferes with the kind of careful listening that guides the work as described by the Kris Study Group. It condemns patients to superficial treatments unless conducted by the very gifted.

In addition, the "borderline" idea is conceptually unnecessary. Had we been faithful to what Freud actually said, had we theorized about *das Ich* or the "I," for example, there would be no place for the concept as it is currently used. We would not have become trapped by the names, the rigid designators, we grafted onto Freud's original thinking. Had we continued to ponder the "I" and the "it," we would have been less likely to lose touch with the their connection to the body that the early ego psychologists grasped. Disregarding Descartes, the pronoun "I," by virtue of its role in language, automatically refers to a speaking *physical* being. Further, had we thought deeply about all that is "Above-I," we would have had a less limited view of what we call "superego." Perhaps we would have maintained Freud's intuition that bodies, gender, object relations, language, and culture can never be treated separately.

And the very notion of "defect" has a familiar smell. Even the blind can detect the "scent of a woman," as the Al Pacino film showed us a few years ago. Freud does bear some responsibility for its role in psychoanalytic theory in that he used the word "defect" in his last statement about women (Freud 1940/1964b, 193). It seems to me that the signifier "defect" holds onto all that nastiness about women that seemed to bleed through Freud's earlier formulations of the feminine superego. Feminists would not tolerate the condemnation of women to an unavoidably flawed moral structure. But the force of the residual misogyny in the theory metonymically shifted the defect to another place, hiding it in the "ego." "A defect in the ego" is another metaphor for the female genital. Or to put it more boldly, the term "borderline" as it is often used, is a euphemism for bitch" or "cunt," a degraded foul female who causes trouble, especially for her therapist. His own explanations aside, Freud probably called Dora "Dora" in his text, because *Dorn* is the German word for "thorn," and Dora was surely a thorn in his side. Some might object that men are diagnosed as "borderline" too. True enough. But most of the patient population so designated is female. And even were that not the case, men so called would simply prove Lacan right. Having a penis does not guarantee that an absent phallus will not leave a hole. The theory "feminizes" certain men as well.

I have learned a lot from the game of golf over the years. Although I have never played, I have spent a lot of time watching the Golf Channel with my husband and now I consider myself an expert. I have learned that a "hole in one" is cause for celebration, and being "below par" is thrilling. The difference between the rough and the green depends on how you cut the grass, and one can be perfectly happy with a handicap. The impulse "to flog" can be refined into an elegant sport simply by spelling it backwards. Had he only known, Freud could have included the game in his essay "The Antithetical Meaning of Primal Words," where he reminded us that we can read language in the same way that we can read our dreams (Freud 1990/1957, 155–61). A careful reading of the language of psychoanalysis may help us to correct our stance.

REFERENCES

Abend, S. M., Porder, M. S., and Willick, M. S. (1983). *Borderline Patients: Psychoanalytic Perspectives*. Madison, CT: International Universities Press.

Bassin, D. (1982). Woman's images of inner space: Data towards expanded interpretive categories. *International Review of Psychoanalysis*, 9, 191–202.

Bernstein, D. (1993). *Female Identity Conflict in Clinical Practice*. N. Freedman and B. Distler, eds. London: Jason Aronson.

Bettelheim, B. (1983). *Freud and Man's Soul*. New York: Knopf.

Boesky, D. (1994). Dialogue on the Brenner paper between Charles Brenner, MD and Dale Boesky, MD. *Journal of Clinical Psychoanalysis*, 3(4), 509–22.

Brenner, C. (1994). The mind as conflict and compromise formation. *Journal of Clinical Psychoanalysis,* 3(4), 473–88.

Brown, L. M. and Gilligan, C. (1992). *Meeting at the Crossroads: Women's Psychology and Girls' Development*. Cambridge, MA: Harvard University Press.

Chodorow, N. J. (1989). *Feminism and Psychoanalytic Theory*. New Haven, CT: Yale University Press.

Deutsch, H. (1944). *The Psychology of Women*. New York: Grune & Stratton.

Ellenberger, H. F. (1970). *The Discovery of the Unconscious: The History and the Evolution of Dynamic Psychiatry*. New York: Basic Books.

Fenichel, O. (1941). *Problems of Psychoanalytic Technique*. D. Brunswick, trans. New York: The Psychoanalytic Quarterly, Inc.

Freud, S. (1953). The interpretation of dreams. In J. Strachey, ed. and trans., *The Standard Edition of the Complete Psychological Works of Sigmund Freud,* Vol. 5. (1–627). London: Hogarth Press. (Original work published 1900)

———. (1957). The antithetical meaning of primary words. In J. Strachey, ed. and trans., *The Standard Edition of the Complete Psychological Works of Sigmund Freud*, Vol. 11 (pp. 155–61). London: Hogarth Press. (Original work published 1910)

———. (1961a). The ego and the id. In J. Strachey, ed. and trans., *The Standard Edition of the Complete Psychological Works of Sigmund Freud*, Vol. 19 (pp. 1–59). London: Hogarth Press. (Original work published 1923)

———. (1961b). The dissolution of the Oedipus complex. In J. Strachey, ed. and trans., *The Standard Edition of the Complete Psychological Works of Sigmund Freud*, Vol. 19 (pp. 173–79). London: Hogarth Press. (Original work published 1924)

———. (1961c). Some psychical consequences of the anatomical distinction between the sexes. In J. Strachey, ed. and trans., *The Standard Edition of the Complete Psychological Works of Sigmund Freud,* Vol. 19 (pp. 241–60). London: Hogarth Press. (Original work published 1925)

———. (1961d). Civilization and its discontents. In J. Strachey, ed. and trans., *The Standard Edition of the Complete Psychological Works of Sigmund Freud*, Vol. 21 (pp. 64–145). London: Hogarth Press. (Original work published 1930 [1929])

———. (1961e). Female sexuality. In J. Strachey, ed. and trans., *The Standard Edition of the Complete Psychological Works of Sigmund Freud,* Vol. 21 (pp. 221–46). London: Hogarth Press. (Original work published 1931)

———. (1964a). On femininity. In J. Strachey, ed. and trans., *The Standard Edition of the Complete Psychological Works of Sigmund Freud,* Vol. 22 (pp. 112–35). London: Hogarth Press. (Original work published 1933)

———. (1964b). An outline of psychoanalysis. In J. Strachey, ed. and trans., *The Standard Edition of the Complete Psychological Works of Sigmund Freud,* Vol. 23 (pp. 139–208). London: Hogarth Press. (Original work published 1940)

Gilligan, C. (1982). *In a Different Voice: Psychological Theory and Women's Development.* Cambridge, MA: Harvard University Press.

Gilligan, C., Lyons, N. P., and Hanmer, T. J. (1990). *Making Connections.* Cambridge, MA: Harvard University Press.

Grob, G. N. (1991). Origins of DSM-I: a study in appearance and reality. *American Journal of Psychiatry*, 148(4), 421–31.

Hartmann, H. (1958). *Ego Psychology and the Problem of Adaptation.* D. Rapaport, trans. New York: International Universities Press. (Original work published 1939)

Heidegger, M. (1962). *Being and Time.* J. Macquarrie and E. Robinson, trans. New York: Harper & Row. (Original work published 1926)

Hite, S. (1976). *The Hite Report.* New York: Macmillan.

Hornblower, S. and Spawforth, A. (1996). *The Oxford Classical Dictionary,* 3rd ed. Oxford: Oxford University Press.

Horney, K. (1950). *Neurosis and Human Growth.* New York: W. W. Norton.

Kalinich, L. J. (1993). On the sense of absence: a perspective on womanly issues. *Psychoanalytic Quarterly*, 52, 206–27.

Kierkegaard, S. (1980). *The Concept of Anxiety.* R. Thomte and A. B. Anderson, eds. and trans. Princeton, NJ: Princeton University Press. (Original work published 1844)

Kripke, S. (1972). *Naming and Necessity.* Cambridge, MA: Harvard University Press.

Lacan, J. (1978). *The Four Fundamental Concepts of Psychoanalysis.* J. A. Miller, ed., A. Sheridan, trans. New York: W.W. Norton & Co.

Mahony, P. J. (1982). A psychoanalytic translation of Freud. In D. E. Ornston, ed., *Translating Freud* (pp. 24–77). New Haven, CT: Yale University Press.

Mayer, E. L. (1995). The phallic castration complex and primary femininity: Paired developmental lines toward female gender identity. *Journal of the American Psychoanalytic Association,* 43, 17–38.

Shengold, L. (1991). *"Father, Don't You See I'm Burning?" Reflections on Sex, Narcissism, Symbolism, and Murder: From Everything to Nothing.* New Haven, CT: Yale University Press.

Stoller, R. J. (1976). Primary femininity. *Journal of the American Psychoanalytic Association*, Supplement, 24, 59–78.

Tyson, P. and Tyson, R. L. (1990). *Psychoanalytic Theories of Development: An Integration.* New Haven, CT: Yale University Press.

Chapter Four

The Lived Body:
From Freud to Merleau-Ponty
and Contemporary Psychoanalysis

Roger Frie, Ph.D., Psy.D.

INTRODUCTION

Psychoanalysis is quite inconceivable without a conception of the human body. More often than not, however, the body is seen only as a way station to "mentalized" experience. Given the traditional Western distinction between the mind and the body, the separation of intellect and soma in psychoanalysis is hardly surprising. Indeed, the problem of the so-called mind-body separation has bedeviled science and philosophy since the seventeenth century, when Descartes questioned the certainty of our bodily experience and ushered his famous dictum, "I think, therefore I am."

The Cartesian dualities of mind and body, subject and object continue to pose challenges for contemporary psychoanalysis, philosophy, and neuroscience alike. In considering the problem of embodiment in psychoanalysis, I draw from each of these disciplines. I focus above all on the phenomenological perspectives on embodiment developed by the French philosopher Maurice Merleau-Ponty (1908–1961) and the Swiss psychiatrist and psychoanalyst Ludwig Binswanger (1881–1966). The work of these thinkers has been integral in bringing about an interdisciplinary discussion of the body (Frie 2003). I argue that Merleau-Ponty's conception of the "lived body" has come closer than most to collapsing the Cartesian duality of mind and body. His philosophy of the lived body demonstrates the way in which understanding, awareness, and communication are all fundamentally embodied. For this reason, I suggest that his ideas are particularly relevant for helping psychoanalysts close the gap between intellect and soma.

My discussion begins with an examination of Freud's contribution to our understanding of the body. I then turn to consider Binswanger and Merleau-Ponty.

After elaborating their key ideas on the body, I suggest ways in which these can be applied clinically and theoretically in order to achieve an "embodied psychoanalysis."

FREUD AND THE BODY

Freud's avowed aim was to create a "science" of psychoanalysis. Early on in his career, Freud (1895/1954) sought to explain the nature of mind in physiological terms, a goal that gave rise to his "Project for a Scientific Psychology." Freud ultimately abandoned his forays in physiological theory building and his "Project" lay dormant until the 1950s, when it was posthumously published. Throughout his career, however, Freud held fast to his belief that eventually human psychology would be explained in physiological terms.

Freud's emphasis on the role of human sexuality in the development of the mind can be understood within his naturalistic paradigm. Freud's search for a physiological foundation upon which to base his burgeoning science of psychoanalysis led him to examine the role of sexuality in human psychology (Sulloway 1979). The importance of sexuality, as a universal, physical phenomenon, had only recently been explored in scientific terms (Krafft-Ebing 1891). By tracing the etiology of his patient's neuroses to their sexual histories, Freud was able to demonstrate the way in which the mind was necessarily linked to the body and its drives.

For Freud, therefore, instinctual drives are first and foremost bodily phenomena. Drives make demands on the mind, which, broadly speaking, attempts to assimilate them. In the terminology of Freud's (1923/1961) structural theory, the ego, as a synthesizing agency of the psyche, seeks to integrate the demands of the blind drives of the id with the exigencies of external reality. The purpose of psychoanalysis, according to Freud, is to facilitate this process.

Freud's emphasis on the body also relates to his conceptualization of the mind. In his famous passage on the ego, Freud declares: "The ego is first and foremost a bodily ego" (Freud 1923/1961, 26). He elaborates the notion of a bodily ego by stating that "the ego is ultimately derived from bodily sensations, chiefly from those springing from the surface of the body" (pp. 26–27). For Freud, therefore, the somatic process that occurs in an organ or part of the body is not only the source of instinctual drives, but also of one's sense of self.

The psyche and drives alike are bodily based phenomena. But does Freud's embrace of the body enable him to avoid the snares of the Cartesian dualism? In an earlier passage, Freud (1915/1957, 22) states that the drives appear as "a measure of the demand made upon the mind for work in consequence of its connection with the body." From this perspective, at least, it is apparent that the body drives the mind. Yet body and mind ultimately remain separate, as Freud's structural theory attests: the ego forever struggles to control and integrate the demands of bodily based drives.

Freud's drive theory has been enshrined, revised, or altogether dismissed by successive generations of psychoanalysts. However, debate over drive theory should not distract us from recognizing the body's clinical importance. Whether one accepts the notion of bodily based drives or seeks to reformulate them (Greenberg 1991), the experience of the body is central to psychological life. Indeed, what Freud's perspective on the ego demonstrates is that the body is fundamental to the construction of the self. The body is not simply a substrate of the mind. Nor is it only the source of endogenous drives and experiences. Rather, the body provides the context for the development of the self and self-experience.

Although Freud's theorizing provided the groundwork for conceptualizing an embodied self, I would suggest that subsequent theory building under the guise of "ego psychology" substantiated the fundamental split between bodily based drives and the role of the ego in the structural theory of mind. Not surprisingly, given its origins in late nineteenth century science, the ego psychological perspective reflects the traditional hierarchical model of the brain, in which the frontal cortex represents the higher functions of the mind, in contrast to the lower components of the brain that control bodily functions. The division of the brain into individual components is important for understanding the physiological nature of the mind. Yet it is an intellectual model that fails to capture actual lived, bodily experience of the patient.

In addition to the separation of mind and body into separate spheres of influence, there is another element at work in psychoanalysis that sustains the mind-body division. Freud's early technique emphasized the importance of free association as a means for the patient to allow his or her unconscious processes to come to the fore. Free association remains a bedrock of classical psychoanalytic technique. There is a problem with this approach, however, since it tends to emphasize language and verbal articulation over the bodily experience. In the process, linguistic articulation is separated from, and seen as implicitly superior to, nonverbal communication and the expression of bodily symptoms. The result is that mind and body are frequently seen as at odds with one another. As Joyce McDougall writes: "Since its inception psychoanalysis, following Freud, has privileged the role of language in the structuring of the psyche and in psychoanalytic treatment. *But not all communications use language.* In attempting to attack any awareness of certain thoughts, fantasies or conflictual situations apt to stir up strong feelings of either a painful or an overexciting nature, a patient may, for example, produce a somatic explosion instead of a thought, a fantasy or a dream" (McDougall 1989, 11; italics in the original).

Indeed, recent psychoanalytic research demonstrates that the traditional psychoanalytic perspective on the intellect versus soma is far more complex. For example, communication has been shown to include such elements as facial expression, gesture, posture, and vocal prosodic elements such as quality of speech, rhythm, and tone (Beebe and Lachmann 1988; Ekman 1993). Research on infant-mother interaction suggests that infants and mothers continually attune to one another's emotional states by matching facial expressions, tone of voice, and behavior. Beatrice Beebe and Frank Lachmann (1988) maintain that when one individual in a dyad matches the other's nonverbal emotion cues, whether body posture or facial expression, that individual recreates the autonomic changes and body sensations associated with the other's emotional state.

When applied to the analytic setting, this research suggests that there is much analytic territory that cannot be defined in terms of free association and interlocution. Indeed, it is probably not too daring to suggest that nonverbal, bodily communication is as important to the analytic process as verbal communication. We need only think about such issues as a patient's facial expression at the beginning or end of a session, the timing and length of silences, or the mood in which interaction is undertaken and achieved to realize that the nonverbal, bodily communication is always implicit in the analytic dyad.

The problem with traditional psychoanalytic theorizing, then, is that it has essentially sanctioned the split between mind and body, intellect and soma. As a result, its theory and technique may appear strangely distant and at odds with both the analyst's and the patient's lived experience. I therefore suggest that we turn to another approach and method, namely, phenomenology, and examine its potential contribution to the problem of embodiment in psychoanalysis.

EMBODIMENT: FROM BINSWANGER TO MERLEAU-PONTY

The notion of embodiment stems from phenomenological philosophy, the aim of which is to describe and identify essential forms of human experience, principally the experience of the body. The application of phenomenology to psychoanalysis was first undertaken by the Swiss psychiatrist and psychoanalyst Ludwig Binswanger, a longtime colleague of Freud. Binswanger and Freud were frequently at odds with one another, yet Freud's interest in Binswanger's career and the latter's desire to learn from his teacher led to a productive exchange of ideas over three decades. Binswanger essentially agreed with Freud's notion of a bodily based ego, maintaining that "the human being not only has a body but is a body and expresses him/herself through the body" (Binswanger 1935, 146). Nevertheless, Binswanger (1936) objected to Freud's tripartite division of the mind and all but rejected the determinism implicit in Freud's theory of drives. He was simply unable to accept the notion that human behavior is causally determined by the instinctual energy of the id. Thus, Binswanger sought to understand and explain human beings in the totality of their existence, not as natural objects constructed from various parts.

In his attempt to place psychoanalysis on a wider footing, Binswanger incorporated the findings of philosophy into his clinical work. Edmund Husserl's project of phenomenology provided him with a method to explain the "visual reality" of the mentally ill person. It was, however, Martin Heidegger's move beyond Husserl in *Being and Time* (1927/1962) that influenced Binswanger's thinking more directly. Heidegger's notion of "being-in-the-world" enabled Binswanger to develop a phenomenological approach to psychiatry that sought to understand the context in which the embodied individual exists and discovers meaning. According to Binswanger, the goal of psychoanalysis is to see how we structure our world and, thus, how we relate to our environment and the people around us.

For Binswanger, the body provides the experiential context for our interaction with the world. Binswanger frequently worked with schizophrenic and psychotic patients, and was attuned to the ways in which they expressed themselves and experienced the world around them through their bodies. Binswanger declared that our bodies form the background for ongoing experience and constitute the very space in which our identities are formed. He argued that our sense of spatial relatedness is reflected in a range of bodily boundaries that can become disturbed pathologically.

The body for Binswanger also provides a means of self-expression. Accordingly, physical symptoms should not be seen merely as a substitution for verbal language, since they constitute a significant form of bodily communication: "One must realize that . . . under certain circumstances [the body] remains the only form of expression left to people, and the human being henceforth also uses the language of the body: that is, instead of scolding and raging, the human being chortles, belches, screeches and vomits" (Binswanger 1935, 146). Moreover, those patients who lacked a verbal capacity for communication relied more visibly on the cognitive capacities of their bodies in order to interact with the world in which they lived. By thus emphasizing the prereflective and preverbal experience of the body, Binswanger sought to develop a concept of embodiment with the aim of overcoming the separation of mind and body in the clinical setting.

The project of embodiment started by Binswanger is fully elaborated in the work of Merleau-Ponty. Like Binswanger, Merleau-Ponty maintains that the mind could only be understood in terms of the body: "The perceiving mind is an incarnated body" (Merleau-Ponty 1962, 3). Whereas Binswanger sought to move beyond Freud by developing a holistic conception of the human being encompassing both mind and body, Merleau-Ponty's specific goal is to collapse once and for all the Cartesian duality of mind and body by arguing that the subject essentially *is* a body. To this end, Merleau-Ponty (1945/1989) introduces the notion of the "body-subject," which draws on Binswanger's earlier (1935) exploration of the same theme. For both thinkers the mind can only be understood in terms of its body and its world. As Merleau-Ponty (1962, 5) notes: "For us the body is much more than an instrument or a means; it is our expression in the world, the visible form of our intentions."

In order to elaborate Merleau-Ponty's theory of embodiment, I examine three key concepts that span the length of his career: the body-subject, reversibility, and flesh. Each of these concepts is complex and must be understood in the larger context of Merleau-Ponty's phenomenological project. My examination, however, will necessarily be limited in scope; for further information, see works by Dillon (1997) and Madison (1981), to which my discussion is indebted.

THE BODY-SUBJECT

Merleau-Ponty's objective in his chief work, *Phenomenology of Perception* (1945/1989), is to study the process of perception in order to overcome the Cartesian duality of mind and body, subject and object. It is by virtue of our embodiment, according to Merleau-Ponty, that we perceive things around us. We can never experience things independent of our bodily existence in the world. Space is always experienced in relation to our bodies as situated in the world. The same is true of time. As embodied beings, we can never be in two places at once. For Merleau-Ponty, therefore, our bodies are a dimension of our very existence.

Merleau-Ponty uses the example of a "phantom limb," in which someone has lost an arm but continues to feel it, to explain the nature of the body-subject. He asserts that the phenomenon of the phantom limb can only be understood from the point of view of a subject for whom the body is indelibly linked to consciousness, to the extent that it forms the very basis for existing within the world. In other words, the subject who experiences the phantom limb is not consciousness that is in some way only attached to a body. On the contrary, consciousness must be understood to be fundamentally embodied.

To feel an arm which one no longer has is "to remain open to all those actions of which the arm alone is capable; it is to keep the practical field that one had before being mutilated" (p. 81). The phantom limb points to the learned bodily schema by which we interact with the world.

For Merleau-Ponty, the lived body is not an object for a subject, but the way in which the subject exists in the world. The perceiving subject is always a worldly, embodied subject. The lived body is not, as Descartes would have us believe, an object in and of itself. Rather, it is the way the subject is present in the world and aware of it. Indeed, the phantom limb points to the existence of a subject intimately bound up with the world through the intentionality of the body.

It is important to note that the perceptual consciousness described by Merleau-Ponty does not constitute an interiority. It is a bodily presence in the world—precisely the means through which conscious awareness of the world is achieved. To be sure, the body has a meaning-bestowing function and in this sense bears a resemblance to Husserl's transcendental ego. But the body does not function as a transcendental ego, as it does for Husserl. It is not an agency underlying the organization of experience, nor is it the foundation of an *a priori* (transcendental) constitution. Moreover, the body does not in and of itself seek to synthesize the world. Rather, it seeks understanding from the bodies with which it interacts. In other words, the body-subject does not constitute the world as horizon of possible experience, but interprets and seeks to understand the world. This brings us to the notion of reversibility.

REVERSIBILITY

According to Merleau-Ponty, the body is a phenomenon situated among other phenomena within the world. Merleau-Ponty argues that my body and yours are not the private, mutually exclusive, solipsistic domains of Cartesian philosophy. Rather, there is a relation of reversibility between the perceiver and the perceived, between the body as sensing and the body as sensed, between my body and yours.

The notion of reversibility, which is central to Merleau-Ponty's ontology, is introduced in his late, unfinished work, *The Visible and the Invisible* (1968). It is prefigured by the notion of "double sensation," of touching and being touched, which is discussed in *Phenomenology of Perception*. Merleau-Ponty uses an everyday example in which I am in the process of touching an object with my right hand, when suddenly my hands cross and I touch my right hand with my left. My right hand, which was touching an object, now becomes touched. At that moment it ceases to be a "sensing" subject and becomes a "sensed" object. The body reflects, or turns back in on itself, and reveals itself as both subject and object. It is, in essence, a two-sided being: subject and object at the same time. The objective of this example of double sensation is to demonstrate the natural reflexivity of the body. In this situation, the body is neither completely a subject nor completely an object. It is, rather, a reversible circularity in which the subject/object distinction is fundamentally blurred.

Merleau-Ponty extends this analysis to the relation of the body and world. The perception of the body is at the same time the perception of the world: "The lived body is in the world as the heart is in the organism; it keeps the visible spectacle constantly alive, it breathes life into it and sustains it inwardly, and with it forms a system" (Merleau-Ponty 1945/1989, 205). Body and world coexist in a dialectical relationship.

In *The Visible and the Invisible*, Merleau-Ponty elaborates the meaning of reversibility. To do so, he returns to his earlier example of "touching." He provides an example in which the interrogator and the interrogated are so close to each other as to be able to touch one another. Merleau-Ponty begins by pointing out that my hand would not be able to sense anything were it not for the fact that it can sense. Therefore, when my hand is able to touch, it is because it is "tangible" and because what is touched can be sensed from the inside. Merleau-Ponty develops a similar argument in regard to vision. Accordingly, I can see precisely because I myself am visible: "he who sees cannot possess the visible unless he is possessed by it, unless he is of it" (Merleau-Ponty 1968, 135). From the same perspective, the body by which I am in the world is itself a part of the world. The lived body and perceived world are correlatives. The point is that the body belongs to the order of both the object and the subject. And it is precisely for this reason that Merleau-Ponty chooses to refer to the body as the flesh.

FLESH

In Merleau-Ponty's later work, then, a revision has taken place. Perception is called vision, and the body itself is referred to as the flesh. The body is no longer just an object of perception, but flesh, a philosophy of "brute being" and the basis of Merleau-Ponty's ontology. Flesh is the formative medium of object and subject. As Merleau-Ponty states: "We must not think the flesh as starting out from substances, from body and spirit—for then it would be the union of contradictories—but we must think it . . . as an element, as the concrete emblem of a general manner of being" (Merleau-Ponty 1968, 147).

In *The Visible and the Invisible*, the act of perception is presented as touching, seeing, and feeling itself. There is no representation at the level of perception. There is only flesh that is in touch with itself. Perception, from this perspective, is a worldly event, not something that occurs privately, since flesh undercuts and precedes the division of subject and object. This has implications for the problem of solipsism as well. According to Merleau-Ponty, the other's world is my world because the two views are reversible. My right hand, being touched by my left, can reverse the roles and touch my left hand back. Similarly, my body, being seen by another person, can reverse roles and take up the other's perspective on itself. The communality between the other and myself is grounded in the flesh that we both visibly are, rather than in the transcendental consciousness I have of that person.

It is through one's own body that one is able to begin to understand the world. Merleau-Ponty argues that we must learn to think of the relation of the body to the world as the relation of flesh to flesh, according to the model of one hand touching another. In other words, flesh refers to the body's capacity of being able to fold in upon itself, its simultaneous orientation to inner and outer. This folding in on itself is decentered because it takes place at a level prior to the emergence of conscious, I-centered personal reflection. It is being that is pre-personal, prior to subject-object differentiation. Thus, subject and object are inherently open to one another, for they are constituted in the flesh.

The radicality of Merleau-Ponty's notion of the flesh exists precisely in his attempt to reconceptualize materialism. The separation of mind and body, subject and object is replaced by the interchangeability and shared participation of touching and tangible, toucher and touched, seer and seen. In Merleau-Ponty's account, lived human experience is a seamless web.

AN EMBODIED PSYCHOANALYSIS

Merleau-Ponty's account of the body-subject and flesh demands that we pay attention to the connectedness and immersion of the body in the world. But how does this fundamental shift in the way we conceptualize the body translate into theory and practice in psychoanalysis? One answer, I suggest, can be found in the way we think about cognition, or understanding. Merleau-Ponty's basic insight that "the perceiving mind is an incarnated body" suggests that our bodies continually provide us with a sense of the situations and contexts in which we exist and interact. This bodily, or felt, sense is not a product of reflective thought. Rather, our bodily sense is prereflective and helps us to orient ourselves and know what we are doing. This "bodily sensing" is neither external observation nor subjective and internal, but a form of interaction. Speaking, in turn, can be said to "carry forward" (Gendlin 1992) our bodily interaction with our environment.

This perspective into the body's cognitive capacity is hardly the select purview of phenomenological philosophy however. Indeed, among neuroscientists currently reflecting on the mind-body problem, Antonio Damasio provides a similar perspective. Damasio argues that the body is a "ground reference" for understanding the world around us: "The body, as represented in the brain, may constitute the indispensable frame of reference for the neural processes that we experience as the mind; that our very organism rather than some absolute external reality is used as the ground reference for the constructions we make of the world around us and for the construction of the ever-present sense of subjectivity that is part and parcel of our experiences; that our most refined thoughts and best actions, our greatest joys and deepest sorrows, use the body as a yardstick" (Damasio 1994, xvi).

In a manner akin to Merleau-Ponty, Damasio is describing the fundamental involvement of the body in all human experience. His insights are particularly germane, since the body, as we know, plays a crucial role in the psychoanalytic dyad.

Current psychoanalytic research illustrates the body's relevance in the treatment of psychic trauma and affective disturbances. Henry Krystal's (1988) work with alexithymic patients suggests that affect is both a mental and bodily phenomenon, which is developed through emotional processing with caregivers. Joyce McDougall (1989) argues that psychoanalysts need to assess psychosomatic disorders because the mind's distress is often evident in somatic manifestations. And feminist psychoanalysts (Benjamin 1995; Harris 1998) demonstrate the importance of the body in the construction of gender and sexual identity. It would seem, therefore, that the patient's bodily existence is always implicit in the discourse of psychoanalytic practice.

Reflecting on Damasio's view of the body, Edgar Levenson proposes that "it may well be that the mind is not master, but is formed and molded by the body . . . [and] that our psychoanalytic desideratum, understanding, is neither entirely verbal nor intellectual, but more a limited reflection on an ineffable felt experience" (Levenson 1998, 240). The notion of felt experience points to the role of affects, which are themselves bodily sensations (Krystal 1988). And, as the psychoanalytic process suggests, affective experience only gradually reaches the point at which it can be articulated or named.

Psychoanalysis has traditionally relied on language: the articulation of thought, affect, fantasy, and dreams in words. I am suggesting that the emphasis on language and the intellect in psychoanalysis implicitly sustains the mind-body separation. As a result, the embodiment of understanding and cognition elaborated by Merleau-Ponty and others remains outside the purview of traditional psychoanalytic theory and practice. According to Merleau-Ponty, our perception and understanding of the world is always and already grounded in our fundamentally embodied selves. He shows us that any attempt to separate intellect and soma is an artificial distinction of a whole. When applied to the psychoanalytic setting, we see that our foundations for self-reflexivity, understanding, and knowledge lie in our bodily sensations and rest in the reversible properties of flesh. Language, in this view, is a necessary, but not sufficient condition of self-awareness (Frie 1999). Rather, we might think of the lived experience in terms of a continual interaction between language and the body. Clearly, whether one accepts or seeks to reformulate Freud's notion of drives, an embodied psychoanalysis must heed the inherent, seamless interactions of intellect and soma, language and body that form the basis of human experience.

REFERENCES

Beebe, B. and Lachmann, F. M. (1988). The contributions of mother-infant mutual influence to the origins of self and object representations. *Psychoanalytic Psychology*, 5, 305–37.

Benjamin, J. (1995). *Like Subjects, Love Objects*. New Haven, CT: Yale University Press.

Binswanger, L. (1935). *Über Psychotherapie*. Ausgewählte Vorträge und Aufsätze, Bd. I. Bern: Francke, 1947.

———. (1936). *Freud's Auffassung des Menschen im Lichte der Anthropologie*. Ausgewählte Vorträge und Aufsätze, Bd. I. Bern: Francke, 1947.

Damasio, A. (1994). *Descartes' Error: Emotion, Reason, and the Human Brain*. New York: Avon Books.

Dillon, M. D. (1997). *Merleau-Ponty's Ontology*. Evanston, IL: Northwestern University Press.

Ekman, P. (1993). Facial expression and emotion. *American Psychologist*, 48, 384–92.

Freud, S. (1954). A project for a scientific psychology. In J. Strachey, ed. and trans., *The Standard Edition of the Complete Psychological Works of Sigmund Freud*, Vol. 1 (pp. 175–243). London: Hogarth Press. (Original work published 1895)

———. (1957). Instincts and their vissicitudes. In J. Strachey, ed. and trans., *The Standard Edition of the Complete Psychological Works of Sigmund Freud*, Vol. 14 (pp.117–40). London: Hogarth Press. (Original work published 1915)

———. (1961). The ego and the id. In J. Strachey, ed. and trans., *The Standard Edition of the Complete Psychological Works of Sigmund Freud*, Vol. 19 (pp. 3–68). London: Hogarth Press. (Original work published 1923)

Frie, R. (1997/2000). *Subjectivity and Intersubjectivity in Modern Philosophy and Psychoanalysis: A Study of Sartre, Binswanger, Lacan, and Habermas*. Lanham, MD: Rowman & Littlefield.

———. (1999). Psychoanalysis and the linguistic turn. *Contemporary Psychoanalysis*, 35, 673–97.

——. (2003). *Understanding Experience: Psychotherapy and Postmodernism*. New York: Routledge.

Gendlin, E. (1992). The primacy of the body, not the primacy of perception. *Man and World*, 25, 341–53.

Greenberg, J. (1991). *Oedipus and Beyond*. Cambridge, MA: Harvard University Press.

Harris, A. (1998). Psychic envelopes and sonorous baths. In L. Aron and F. Sommer Anderson, eds., *Relational Perspectives on the Body* (pp. 39–64). Hillsdale, NJ: The Analytic Press.

Heidegger, M. (1962). *Being and Time*. Oxford: Blackwell. (Original work published 1927)

Krafft-Ebing, R. (1891). *Neue Forschungen auf den Gebeit der Psychopathia sexualis: eine medicinish-psychologische Studie*. Stuttgart: F. Enke.

Krystal, H. (1988). *Integration and Self-Healing*. Hillsdale, NJ: The Analytic Press.

Levenson, E. (1998). Awareness, insight, learning. *Contemporary Psychoanalysis*, 34, 239–49.

Madison, G. B. (1981). *The Phenomenology of Merleau-Ponty*. Athens: Ohio University Press.

McDougall, J. (1989). *Theaters of the Body: A Psychoanalytic Approach to Psychosomatic Illness*. New York: Norton.

Merleau-Ponty, M. (1962). *The Primacy of Perception*. Evanston, IL: Northwestern University Press.

——. (1968). *The Visible and the Invisible*. Evanston, IL: Northwestern University Press.

——. (1989). *Phenomenology of Perception*. London: Routledge. (Original work published 1945)

Sulloway, F. (1979). *Freud: Biologist of the Mind*. Cambridge, MA: Harvard University Press.

Chapter Five

Identificatory Channels in Psychosis: Mimicry as Adhesion and Mockery as Differentiation

Jane G. Tillman, Ph.D.

INTRODUCTION

In this chapter I examine the developmental trajectories of mimicry and mockery, using an extended clinical case report of intensive treatment of a patient with schizophrenia, and a review of salient aspects of the literature on these constructs. Mimicry and mockery are within the repertoire of social behavior in normal and psychopathological development—they exist on a continuum, involving expressive use of bodily activity. I developed an interest in this topic through clinical experience, particularly in my work with a schizophrenic young man, seen four times per week, in face-to-face, individual sessions over the course of nearly six years. The setting for this work is a small psychiatric hospital devoted to the study and treatment of severe psychopathology. In addition to intensive psychotherapy, immersion in a therapeutic community program provides an additional holding environment and learning context for the treatment. I treated other schizophrenic patients during this time and saw other instances of both mimicry and mockery. As with certain character disordered patients struggling to use their aggression, mockery becomes a not infrequent event in the treatment, used to ward off impingement or fears of internalizing a destructive object.

I will use various aspects of the psychoanalytic canon to explicate my understanding of the clinical phenomena I observed in my patient. Lacanian theory, as explicated by Muller (1996, 2000), provides a useful framework for understanding registers of human experience, and has been particularly useful to me in working with psychotic patients. For Lacan, human experience falls into three general registers. The *Real* is Lacan's term for a region of unnamable scatter and disorganization. There is no past or future, no language, only immediacy of experience without a mediating structure. Such a state of dedifferentiation often results from a severe dissociative response to trauma. Muller (2000) describes the Real as "beyond an epistemological frontier, that aspect of experience without a name and without an image" (p. 51). This is the dimension of psychosis. In contrast to the undifferentiated Real, the *Imaginary* register includes moving into mastery, unity, coherence, mirroring, hate and love, one-to-one correspondence, disavowal, illusion, and alienation. This is the field of "enacted iconicity" (Johansen 1993 quoted in Muller 2000). Transference enactments occurring in the Imaginary register often occur through coerced mirroring, where one member of the therapeutic dyad uses affect to captivate the other member of the pair. Ideally, such captivation is shared and fluid, not falling into a totalitarian frame of relations. I suggest that in some cases, mimicry is one way to build a bridge from the undifferentiated Real of psychosis, to the Imaginary of dyadic relations.

Finally, the *Symbolic* register is a place of mediated relations, plurality, differentiation, trust, integrity, and shared understanding. Language becomes meaningful beyond concrete naming of things in the room. Social custom, law, grammar, ritual, and shared meaning systems are evident here. The Symbolic register is represented by the Third, the witness to the truth, and a place from which two-party contracts and treaties are judged. In this framework, mockery stands as a double defense: against moving into the Symbolic order as a developmental progression from the dyad to triads, or against further regression, since mockery may also intervene to preserve a bodily caricature of the dyad in order to stave off a return to frank psychosis.

CLINICAL EXAMPLE

My patient, Nathaniel, was raised primarily by his father after his parents divorced when he was three years old. Nathaniel was lonely in childhood, odd, socially anxious, and either ignored or occasionally bullied. Both mother and father had extensive substance abuse histories, most active during Nathaniel's young life, and now in apparent remission. Additionally, his mother had problems with self-harm and an eating disorder. All of these parental difficulties contributed to an atmosphere of neglect for Nathaniel. In adolescence, Nathaniel developed a severe drinking problem, that he told me was, in part, to establish that he "was better than" his parents and could handle his drinking. This form of imitation of adulthood, through drinking, as well as mockery of his parents' weakness and authority was embedded in his reasoning about his drinking. At his boarding school Nathaniel was brutally teased by dorm residents who found him odd, scary, and a drunken nuisance. He did not attend class, could not get organized, and became a social outcast—something enraging and humiliating to him, but which he was unable to develop a perspective about because he could not tolerate self-reflective activity. His description led me to think that the only mirror available to Nathaniel was one transmitting his parents' brokenness and initiating his cycle of mimicry and mockery.

Away from home, Nathaniel continued to drink and developed torturous paranoid ideation in which he believed he was being followed by malevolent figures. He was eventually expelled from school and returned home to his father. Unable to manage his temper, Nathaniel became enraged when his father left on business trips and would not provide continuous care for him. A power struggle ensued over meals—Nathaniel feeling that it was the father's solemn duty to keep food in the house at all time, while the father was giving Nathaniel money to go to the grocery store to shop for food himself. This resulted in a twenty-five pound weight loss for Nathaniel who refused to go to the store for food. He instead spent money on alcohol and continued to drink, hallucinate and deteriorate. His anger about not being taken care of by his father was enormous; he eventually assaulted his father and the police were called. In this context Nathaniel came for hospital treatment and we began our work together.

In the first year of treatment, Nathaniel was disorganized and not very verbal. He seemed lost in critical ways. He had trouble making it to his appointments and never quite knew what day it was or what time it was. Simple suggestions like purchasing a watch, or using a calendar, were of little use to him. Calendars and watches are concrete markers of the Symbolic register and as such promote differentiation. He relied on me to call him to come for his appointments and other patients to come get him for meals. Nathaniel became a mascot of sorts; many women took him on as a surrogate son—in his first year of treatment various older female patients took it upon themselves to take him for haircuts, help him clean his room, and do his laundry. In essence he was a very young boy, grandiose in his entitled expectation that adults take care of him, and stubbornly passive. Despite assistance from a caseworker, he could not tolerate school and would not work individually with a tutor. For a time, he was content to be adopted by other patients as a child, a status that eventually left him feeling more demeaned than cared for.

Nathaniel was often psychotic in the sessions, with paranoid ideation and numerous fears about harm coming to him. In this first year of treatment, mimicry was often a feature of our time together. Without coherent spoken language, his mimicry of me and occasionally of other patients seemed rather innocuous and sad. Speaking so as to approximate my dialect, or dressing in the manner of other patients out of a wish to be included, Nathaniel's mimicry was empty in nature, and shifted to accommodate changes in circumstance. This mimicry did not seem to be in the service of internalization or identification; rather it was momentary adaptation to whatever or whoever was in his immediate field. The quality of Nathaniel's presentation was of being lost, both temporally and spatially. Nathaniel's gestural approximations of the other in his visual field were forms of configuring himself in concrete bodily fashion, by relying on the other's body for the creation of a self.

My patient was extraordinarily stubborn, often in a self-defeating mode, refusing many treatment recommendations including prescribed antipsychotic medication. His passive refusal involved repeated "forgetting" and confusion; he seemed impervious to the latent aggression in his actions. More often than not Nathaniel had access to a tremendous sadness, and remarkably, when sad, his thinking was quite clear with periods of secondary process in evidence. I think this is what made our attachment so strong: he could evoke an overwhelming sadness in me that was a signifier of effective projective identification, a hopeful sign in the treatment as it requires some capacity in both parties of the dyad for affective resonance. The value of such resonance was that I became aware of his skillful and powerful capacity for producing iconic enactments in me. I also found myself irritated with his eternal slowness and disorganization, but did not recognize this anger in me as also unconscious projective identification; instead I thought it was conscious provocation on his part.

Toward the end of the first year of treatment, as my first lengthy vacation (two weeks) approached, Nathaniel's drinking escalated, and for the first time he moved from his passive status to that of an aggressive and threatening young man. In the context of others fearing that he could become assaultive when drinking alcohol, and his inability to maintain his sobriety, he was transferred to another hospital with a locked ward for several weeks of intensive substance abuse treatment. While extremely angry about this recommendation, he did assent to the transfer in an effort to preserve his treatment in the hospital and with me. The patient, however, could not claim his own joining this recommendation, feeling that he was being forced by an immense power to submit to unneeded treatment. Nathaniel was readmitted after my vacation with the understanding that he would work on maintaining his sobriety in order to preserve his treatment. This second phase of our work, lasting over four years, brought into the treatment the move from mimicry to mockery.

In the two-week separation, and with his feeling that I had not "stood up" for him to hospital authority regarding the issue of his transfer, Nathaniel felt humiliated, frightened and rageful. The unfortunate enactment was that I had surrendered him to the paternal authority of the hospital—necessary for the salvaging of his treatment and resulting in a profound dynamic shift for the remainder of his treatment. Mockery, sarcasm, devaluation, and anger became the hallmark of the treatment. Where the patient had passively refused many aspects of the treatment in the first year, his passivity was now suffused with more obvious aggression. He rejected medication, ignored groups, and refused to come speak with the treatment team. Again, he could not tolerate looking at how his own behavior led to the very painful consequences of the transfer. Acknowledging that any external standard (functioning as a Third to the dyad) had a legitimate claim on the two of us was simply out of the question. Such an acknowledgment of any law beyond the dyad was too threatening and unfortunately premature (as was separation from the original maternal dyad). For this patient to accede to external claims was to risk losing his frail sense of autonomy and thereby collapse into dedifferentiation, and such a state only aggravated his profound paranoia about an impending destruction.

I think the trauma of the transfer evoked the memory of the early rupture of the maternal dyad, when my patient felt abandoned in a period of oral need, and not well cared for. The imposition of a Third in the form of hospital authority, boundaries, policies, treatment guidelines, and so forth, all disturbed what had become a deeply dyadic treatment. This necessary appearance of the Third, unconsciously called forth by the patient's drinking, resulted in a deep grievance for the patient, who felt both the maternal abandonment (my vacation), and the paternal authority forcing premature separation. Such a confluence repeated the neglect of his childhood as well as the helplessness of Nathaniel and his maternal object to provide a good-enough solution in the face of separation conflicts. In his psychosis, Nathaniel was unable to appreciate his contribution to the recreation of this early trauma. For him, the repetition was a nightmare in which he again had no agency, although in the contemporary situation this was because he refused his agency. His emptying the enactment of meaning or motivation rendered this repetition a form of mimicry. The aggressive retaliation in the face of his hurt became a transference element suffusing the dyad in painful ways in the years ahead. In the first year of the treatment, the depth of the attachment had been underground for the patient as he worked to emerge from the Real of psychosis into the Imaginary of the dyad through his mimicry. The humiliation of the temporary loss of his treatment highlighted the depth of the attachment and created unbearable states of arousal, need, fear, counterdependence, disgust and self-loathing. Once my patient became aware that the dyad he had worked hard to enter through mimicry (iconic mastery) was subject to the Third, a new set of conflicts emerged.

A simple example of this was how my standard greeting of "hello" when the patient entered the room was now met with a ritualized response of "very much, thank you." In this moment, social rupture by an unmatched response announced the opening move of discontinuity that continued throughout the treatment. My speech, signifying my solidarity with social convention, was to be resisted at each step through violations of social grammar, avoidance or at times verbal attack. Silence on my part in the beginning of the session disrupted this important ritual and was often felt to be hostile. I asked Nathaniel about his apparently unmatched response to "hello" and he said, "I don't know what you are talking about." What does such a refusal accomplish? It maintains a type of omnipotence and perhaps keeps the door to the Real open for the therapist. An advantage to keeping this door open, through the trashing of the social compact, allows the patient to expose his psychotic position, displaying to the therapist the original trauma so that the opportunity for social linkage might occur (Davoine 1981). I think at the same time it preserved a space for private grammar in our therapeutic dyad. I certainly would not repeat our private ritual elsewhere, nor would the patient's behavior be well tolerated by others who would generally throw up their hands in exasperation and leave him alone.

The most striking aspect of this second portion of the treatment was the patient's contorted facial grimacing, his abrupt threatening motions—best described as head fakes—his rageful "stare down" tactics, and his exaggeration of even slight facial expressions on my part. Grimacing, echopraxia, echolalia, and negativism of this sort have been identified as standard symptoms of schizophrenia. Such a shift as this was very disconcerting for me, for I was often watching my patient essentially "ape" my every facial move and gesture twentyfold—the experience was like being in the room with a grotesque caricature of myself. Subtle mimicry that had once been of benign interest to me was now glaring iconic mockery and generated a heightened affective arousal in me. It was like seeing a monstrous bodily reflection of aspects of my body not ordinarily in my awareness. The countertransference affect was to be dehumanized, humiliated and acutely aware of my every move, eventually useful, I think, for developing some empathy for my patient's lifelong plight. On several occasions, when Nathaniel was engaged in these facial gymnastics, he angrily accused *me* of mocking *him*, highlighting the self/other boundary disturbance. I asked about the new symptoms of grimacing and head faking and the patient quickly and angrily replied, "You are crazy, I don't know what you are talking about." It soon became clear to me that I was not to look at Nathaniel directly, because this stirred an intolerable fragmentation and then aggression in him and a tremendous discomfort in me. I tried to speak to him about this but he would have none of it. It was as if the hopes for benign mirroring were dashed and a cruel, vengeful, freak show reflection had taken its place.

We settled into several years of avoidance, and attempts to engage this through talk or a rare interpretation were futile. My interpretations sought to convey to Nathaniel that I understood his fear that he might be controlled by me, or that he might be worried about his limited ability to control me. I linked this to his unpredictable and explosive father, with whom he felt so little self-control, and his fear of his father's own lack of self-control. The trauma of the previous transfer was also in this discourse, a place where his out-of-control drinking had led to a powerful authority stepping in to assert some control for him. Returning to the topic of his drinking and the subsequent hospitalization in an alcoholism unit inevitably angered the patient, who would rail about how unfairly he had been treated, leading to escalating mockery. I eventually worried that I was avoiding my patient, refusing to look at him because of as yet unknown consequences, although my feeling was that these could be dire. The unarticulated prohibition was worsened by the refusal of coherent speech that so often marked the patient's stance. Deprived of my linguistic entitlement to speak, interpret, or exchange meaningful verbal communication about this behavior, I was left to read the bodily surface of my patient's movements through projection, clinical inference, fantasy, and other methods that did not seem quite reliable to me. I worried for some time that I was *refusing* the transference by acceding to his coercive demand, yet I was aware that to do otherwise was to risk *enacting* a transference about which I knew very little.

Interestingly, during this time, Nathaniel took on the dress of a punk rocker, with purple hair, tattoos, piercings, and black leather clothing. After entering a relationship with a young woman who enjoyed this fashion, he adopted this look with her help. Residing in our small New England village, he was certainly inviting others to stare at him, to look, and to notice. In part this was helpful to Nathaniel, who now had a way of understanding why people were looking at him, beyond his otherwise paranoid projections. He felt more in control now because his fantasies about his own psychological oddity were contained in his dress and thus somewhat externalized and understandable. This also gave him license to stare back, in a menacing fashion, as if to defend his right to exist.

In the treatment, coherent speech was rare and often included angry diatribes about all of the injustices he felt were being visited upon him by malevolent figures, or fantastic theories he constructed about the origin of the galaxy. More direct transference interpretations about his anger and confusion with me were contemptuously dismissed, and attempts to help the patient understand something about his own contributions to his situation were angrily refused. The avoidance of looking at one another and my attempts to think out loud about this with Nathaniel were generally unsuccessful. One day I decided to experiment by holding my gaze. This was a disaster. Nathaniel and I became locked in a mutual gaze that was stubborn, intense, and eventually led to rage in my patient who exploded with a number of paranoid accusations that I was a Nazi. Mocking my speech he stood, raising his right hand and yelling, "Heil Hitler," then angrily left the session. In this moment, he projected his own awareness that he was behaving like a Nazi into me, reexperiencing this projection as coming from me. Feeling controlled by his behavior, I acted out my concern that I was avoiding him through coerced gaze aversion. About thirty minutes after storming out of the session Nathaniel telephoned, frightened that he had damaged me and concerned for my welfare. In this call both of us seemed relieved to find the other reconstituted in some familiar fashion.

An episode of this intensity was never repeated in the treatment. Both Nathaniel and I had some understanding of the code of not looking and of Nathaniel's wish not to be seen as fragmented and fractured, or inhabiting the register of the Real, something that direct looking intimately exposed. The direct contact activated intolerable aggression in Nathaniel, which he then projected into me and experienced as my aggression attacking him through my look. His difficulty being seen on this psychotic frontier was a defense against humiliation, but also prevented him from fully entering the sphere of dyadic relations, the province of the Imaginary register. Over the remaining year of the treatment I spoke with Nathaniel about this particular moment in the treatment, letting him know that I understood a bit of the problem he faced when facing himself, namely, that he was in an ongoing state of torment about the condition of his mind, his developmental stall, and the peril he felt when exposed to the direct gaze of the other, a gaze that could defeat his wish to conceal his damage. With much effort and ambivalence, about eight months after the session described above, he left the treatment to live closer to his father. Homesick for some time, Nathaniel felt that he needed to be in more familiar surroundings in order to feel welcomed and somewhat secure.

DISCUSSION

The channel for iconic projective identification, opened by the experiment, stimulated the patient's fears about the uncontainable nature of his aggression, and the aggression he felt emanating from the maternal gaze produced fears of rejection and abandonment. Nathaniel experienced my direct gaze as an active refusal to contain my own curiosity about looking, breaking our private code of conduct, and my naiveté about the obvious danger this posed to him. I surmise that my direct gaze was experienced by the patient as engaging aggressively in coercive mirroring and capturing his affect such that he felt overstimulated and directly challenged in this disorganizing iconic storm, one allowing me to see his psychic destruction directly. The episode illuminated some of the aims of the patient's use of mimicry and mockery which I now understood to be, in part, directed at closing iconic channels of exchange by controlling and distorting the contributions of the other, such that the patient could feel protected from the vicissitudes of aggression and the humiliation of being seen as a shattered mirror, rather than his lifelong wish to be seen as "normal." The coercive gesture on his part, that I never "look," was a wish for normalization on his part, an illusory status he hoped would spare himself and the other the full weight of his unbearable state of mind.

The session of direct looking qualifies for what Caper (1999) refers to as "experimental disasters in psychotic states." Noting that the psychotic person projects into his objects from a place of intense confusion about inner and outer reality, Caper observes that the act of projecting in this state of mind produces its own trauma: "For such a person, a projection into the object is not a test probe, it is something that he feels turns the object into the projection, that engulfs the object and infiltrates its every pore . . . this eliminates the possibility of learning about the object through projective probing" (p. 88). Here the helpful developmental strategy of imitation, or useful mutual iconic projective probing, deteriorates into intolerable confusion, rendering the process frightening and without much hope for producing learning. In this moment, mockery may arise in order to mobilize an aggressive control of the object through dehumanization. I now turn to a discussion of mimicry, caricature, and mockery as developmental and clinical phenomena.

Mimicry

Mimesis is the approximation of the gestures, speech, or the dress of another. It is a normal process observed in everyday life and is a part of infant development (Stern 1990, 61). Research indicates that infants between twelve and twenty-one days can imitate both the facial and manual gestures of an other; this type of mimicry addresses the question of "what can I do?," a question about gestural mastery. Meltzoff and Moore (1999) propose a theory of Active Intermodal Mapping (AIM) to explain how imitation occurs at such an early age. Through experimental observational research, infants are understood to accomplish their imitative gestures through a matching-to-target process (p. 152). The next question is: Why imitation? Again, Meltzoff and Moore note: "Infants deploy imitation to probe whether an encounter with a person is a re-encounter with a familiar person or a new encounter with a stranger. Using imitation for this purpose serves a social-identity function . . . infants treat a person's nonverbal behavior as an identifier of who the individual is, and use imitation as a means of verifying this identity. The fundamental idea is that the distinctive behavior and special interactive games of people serve as markers of their identity" (p. 153).

In the 1970s researchers believed that early imitation was specialized, and was different from and perhaps even unrelated to later imitation. More recent findings suggest that imitation does not drop out but undergoes rapid change with different goals. I propose using the term mimicry to denote these earlier gestural forms, and imitation to describe those behaviors addressed at social identity. In this early activity, mimicry is aimed toward something similar to Winnicott's (1958) theory of motility as establishing unit status and bodily capacities.

At about six weeks the infant is using facial expressions to explore questions about the identity of the other. Promoting the beginning of self/other distinctions, this is the beginning of a dyadic adventure. Fourteen-month-olds recognize that the responsive play of adults with them is a "matching game" and "test whether they are being copied by abruptly changing acts while staring at the adult to see what he/she will do" (Meltzoff and Moore, 1997, 189). For Meltzoff and other researchers, imitation is seen as a discovery procedure for understanding persons. My patient's head fakes and sudden lunges may have been in the neighborhood of this later identity exploration, attempting to leave the captivating space of the other and to establish some type of independent semiotic authority.

In psychotic patients, the flatness of the performance and the unconscious dimensions of mimicry often occur at the presymbolic and therefore preinterpretive level. Mimicry in the psychotic patient shares some of the features Tustin (1984) observes in autistic development. In this psychopathological condition, repetitive mimicry does not enjoy the developmental thrust seen in normal infant growth, for here the transition to internalization and subsequent identification are not achieved and the mimicry remains a concrete response to the body surface of the object in the room. Bick (1968) notes that unintegrated children feel that their skin is adhesive, such a perception forestalling the horror of falling apart, leaking, or further disintegrating. In this condition, mimicry may seek to stabilize a fragmented mind through simple gestural approximation, an activity binding primitive anxieties.

The process of psychosis, different in many ways from primary autism, may recapitulate some of the same integrative/disintegrative features observed in primitive development. In the psychotic arena, mimicry may represent a form of regression that does not readily progress toward internalization or identity formation. This leads to chronicity and contributes to the social disorganization and lonely isolation of many schizophrenic patients.

Treating these patients requires the use of presymbolic channels: prosody of the therapist's voice, attention to one's facial expressions or movement, periodicity of appointments and rituals, and other aspects of the treatment discovered by the patient as essential for establishing continuity of experience and self-cohesion. Mimicry here may be an iconic grafting by the patient onto the observable body surface of the therapist as a grid for structuring cohesiveness.

The body surface of the therapist may be used as an autistic object with mimicry that is not fully related to the therapist as a person, but as a deanimated moving object or container. This is reminiscent of the description of infants at six weeks of age, trying to establish their agency and ability to move and act with some established regularity. The echopraxia and echolalia of psychosis may represent the attempt to find an adhesive surface for establishing a boundary at the Real. Mimicry may also represent a resistance in the psychotic patient to the task of internalization and identification, because internalization activates paranoid fear of control that in turn leads the patient to repetitively expel the object. Nathaniel was working in this arena until the reality of my vacation disrupted the evolving synchronicity of time and ritual, contributing to his rage fueled by the self-destructive protest of drinking and threatened violence.

Mockery

A developmental corollary to mimicry is caricature, used by both children and adults to magnify and thus more reliably identify affect states. Researchers have demonstrated that caricatured faces are more rapidly recognized than veridical faces (Mauro and Kubovy 1992; Rhodes, Byatt, Tremewan, and Kennedy 1997). The theory underlying this finding is that exaggeration of the deviations of a face found in caricature emphasizes distinctive features that are encoded by the subject. Referred to as superportraits, caricatures are found to be capable of eliciting not only more rapid but also more accurate recognition than veridical faces (Mauro and Kubovy 1992). Thus facial exaggerations of emotions on posters or in cartoons allow children to begin to identify affect states and provide the cues for both children and adults to decode facial information with greater rapidity and accuracy.

The range of caricature is wide, producing survival advantages of rapid decoding of facial information, providing some of our best humor and, when suffused with too much aggression, may reach the form of mockery. If mimicry in its pathological form is in the realm of resistance to internalization, then at its furthest reach, mockery can be thought of as an active defeating process (Cooperman 1979), or the chewing up and spitting out of the primary object. What is defeated in this stance may be the Third, the synchrony of the dyad, or the integrity of speech. Janet Miller (1998) refers to "hostile mimicry" as a form of identification with the aggressor. I think "hostile mimicry" is an apt description of the evolution of mimicry, but suggest preserving the term mockery for distinctive purposes. Primitive forms of mockery represent the attempt to use aggression to protect oneself from engulfment, impingement or humiliation by diminishing the perceived power and threat of the other. However, mockery may also preserve the object relationship, because the other is needed to provide the material for caricature (Procci 1987).

Caricature in everyday life, at its most effective, involves the sublimation of aggression and may reach the form of humor—witness our fascination with political satire, often an exercise in the caricature of authority. Less sublimated aggression results in a type of mockery directed at the ongoing humiliation of the weak, reminding such persons that they have little power and are not worthy of full humanity or social membership. Our treatment of the poor and disenfranchised often produces a more aggressive and cruel form of mockery. These are examples of the social forms of mockery readily played out in our public life. Other forms of mockery attack the Symbolic order of custom, culture, or other holding structures beyond the dyad.

The bidirectional field of mockery includes the capacity to diminish the powerful, as well as to humiliate the weak. Mockery does not appear as an expectable moment in early childhood, but becomes more prominent as the latency child enters the social world of sibling rivalry, competition, and social interaction. The appearance of the capacity to mock is displayed in forms of schoolyard bullying and certainly in adolescence with the attempt to achieve independence while negotiating the conflicts arising out of encounters with authority. Anna Freud (1946) notes that identification with the aggressor is "one of the ego's most potent weapons in its dealings with external objects which arouse anxiety" (p. 110). The perversions may include an element of mockery in order to preserve a space for gratification through action. Transferences involving extreme forms of mockery require an understanding that the terrors of identification have been aroused, and that the patient feels compelled to ward off the internalization necessary for identification because of persecutory fears. Here, mockery represents a defense against moving forward into mutuality, but also marks a place of differentiation, forestalling a return to the Real, or undifferentiated psychosis. In figure 5.1, I offer a diagram of this process to clarify my thinking.

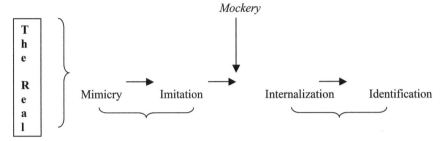

Figure 5.1

Psychosis is not a temporal regression to an earlier developmental level. Psychosis is an odd mixture of abilities achieved, altered, distorted, changed, fragmented, reassembled, and deployed with varying levels of disturbance or distortion. In this state of fragmentation, the familiar strategies of early basic self/other regulation may be revived in an effort to reestablish the identity of self and other. In the psychotic patient, mimicry is not the simple replication of an earlier process, but the application of earlier methods to new and untenable conditions. Likewise, the survival advantage implied in the caricature research may be distorted under the sway of paranoid fears and the aggression accompanying such fears, giving way to mockery and gross distortions of self and other.

If this psychotic netherworld can be approached with all of the means at our disposal, then the move toward an outside material world of objects and independent persons may come to be tolerated and the mental mechanisms of defense may supplant iconic enactment. Internalization may gradually become less of a catastrophic threat and relating to the other as a human subject may become possible. While mockery may establish a boundary against the pull toward nebulous iconicity, the long-term deployment of this defense may lead the treatment into a developmental stall. At its best, for the psychotic patient the aggression required for mockery demarcates the good-me, bad-me, not-me states; inside and outside, self/other, love/hate and other achievements of splitting through categorization and sorting. However, this state of affairs is still quite primitive and does not engage the language of speaking, allowing words to stand for things or ideas, the hallmark symbolic capacity making interpretation possible.

REFERENCES

Bick, E. (1968). The experience of the skin in early object relations. *International Journal of Psychoanalysis*, 49, 484–86.

Caper, R. (1999). *A Mind of One's Own*. London: Routledge.

Cooperman, M. (1979). A possible development in psychoanalytic psychotherapy, and some caveats. *Journal of the National Association of Private Psychiatric Hospitals*, 10(4).

Davoine, F. (1981). A Lacanian Case. Paper presented at the Austen Riggs Center, Stockbridge, MA.

Freud, A. (1946). *The Ego and the Mechanisms of Defense*. Oxford: International Universities Press.

Mauro, R. and Kubovy, M. (1992). Caricature and face recognition. *Memory and Cognition,* 20, 433–40.

Meltzoff, A. N. and Moore, M. K. (1997). Explaining facial imitation: A theoretical model. *Early Development and Parenting*, 6, 179–82.

———. (1999). Resolving the debate about early imitation. In A. Slater and D. Muir, eds., *Developmental Psychology* (pp. 151–55). Oxford: Blackwell Publishers.

Meltzer, D. (1975). Adhesive identification. *Contemporary Psychoanalysis,* 11, 289–310.

Miller, J. (1998). The enemy inside: An exploration of the defensive processes of introjecting and identifying with the aggressor. *Psychodynamic Counseling*, 4(1), 55–70.

Muller, J. P. (1996). *Beyond the Psychoanalytic Dyad*. New York: Routledge Press.

———. (2000). Hierarchical models in semiotics and psychoanalysis. In J. P. Muller and J. Brent, eds., *Peirce, Semiotics, and Psychoanalysis* (pp. 49–67). Baltimore, MD: The Johns Hopkins University Press.

Procci, W. R. (1987). Mockery through caricature: A variant of introjection utilized by a masochistic woman. *Journal of the American Academy of Psychoanalysis,* 15, 51–66.

Rhodes, G., Byatt, G., Tremewan, T., and Kennedy, A. (1997). Facial distinctiveness and the power of caricatures. *Perception,* 26, 207–23.

Stern, D. (1990). *Diary of a Baby*. New York: Basic Books.

Tustin, F. (1984). Autistic shapes. *International Review of Psychoanalysis,* 11, 279–90.

Winnicott, D. W. (1958). Aggression in relation to emotional development. In *Through Paediatrics to Psychoanalysis* (pp. 204–18). New York: Basic Books.

Chapter Six

Containment and the Use of the Skin

Donna M. Elmendorf, Ph.D.

Patients who engage in repetitive self-mutilation present enormous challenges. They often present with chaotic behavior, rely on action over words, and struggle in psychotherapy because of profound impoverishment of fantasy, associations, memories, and affect. This chapter draws on the treatment of a woman, referred for inpatient care for malignant, dissociated self-mutilation, to illustrate the clinical usefulness of a developmental framework regarding the skin. Extending the arguments of those who suggest that repetitive deep cutting is an attempt to return to a fantasized oneness with the maternal object (Tillman 1999; Woodruff 1999), I indicate how an object relations developmental perspective can provide a vantage point from which to view the disturbing, disorienting symptom of self-mutilation. I emphasize the relationship of early dyadic processes to the physical and psychological experience of owning and living in the body and illustrate how my patient developed a set of defenses against the anxiety of failed dependency, imminent self-fragmentation, and the deficit in her capacity for self-soothing. With this patient, the vicissitudes of a disturbed symbiotic phase were reflected in her self-mutilation and accompanying symptoms, and were concretized in the transference. I hope to illustrate how reflection on the earliest phases of mother-infant relatedness can provide support for the therapist faced with such troubled and troubling patients.

Christine, a fifty-four-year-old single woman, was referred for an inpatient evaluation of her recurrent self-mutilation that had resulted in multiple previous hospitalizations with little impact. I worked with her for five months in four-times-weekly psychoanalytically oriented psychotherapy until she returned home to treatment with her outpatient therapist. Her cutting, which almost always required sutures, occurred only during dissociative episodes, marked by drinking, sexual liaisons with strangers, aggressive outbursts, and buying sprees. Typically, her self-mutilation ended these episodes, bringing her back to awareness. She would not remember anything leading up to the cutting but would "come to" and realize she was bleeding. Christine was a middle child in a poor family of seven. Sexually abused by family members as a child, she had been raped as an adult. She had an extremely limited capacity to speak about her life in language that would adequately reflect its horror.

CONTAINER AND CONTAINED

The development of the capacity to symbolize experience occurs in the context of the early mother-infant dyad. Bion (1962) suggests that the mother takes in the infant's chaotic somatic, sensory states through "reverie," a maternal state which is both somatic and cognitive. The infant's dysphoric, non-verbal communications to the mother induce in her (through a primitive form of projective identification) a reflection of the infant's distressed state. Her adult capacities allow her to locate her affective reaction in the context of her knowledge about her own and her infant's body. This then permits her to transform her infant's distress into something thinkable and less somatically disorganized and disorganizing. The mother communicates her containment and calm back to the infant through her touch, voice, and gaze and through her care of the infant's body. This process of giving structure to the chaotic is what Bion (1962) refers to as "containment," conceptualizing the mother as container and the infant as contained. Over time, with repeated experience of this process, the infant develops a capacity to transform the chaotic into the manageable, and ultimately the somatic into the thinkable (Winnicott 1971). That is, the developing child gradually takes in the mother's capacity to contain.

If the mother is stirred by her infant in a way that she herself cannot contain, instead of offering back to the infant a metabolized version of the infant's experience, she may induce in the infant her own reactive affect. In such cases, the infant is faced with the *mother's* experience rather than the mother's reflection of the baby's experience. This process is, of course, problematic for the developing infant. First, the infant is deprived of the mother's containing context, thereby interfering with the infant's developing capacity to recognize and symbolize her own feeling states. Second, through receiving a reflection of affect that is either unrelated to the infant's experience, or a version of that experience distorted by the mother's own unbearable affect, the infant is vulnerable to both a "disturbing sense of otherness" (Fonagy and Target 2000) and, more seriously, a threat to self-cohesion. The opportunity for the child to experience and integrate her own affect, modified by the mother's soothing touch and relevant language, is lost. The repetition of this process leaves the developing child unable to symbolize, and excessively tied to the physical and concrete.

Winnicott (1960) notes that a central aspect of self-cohesion that evolves out of this early mother-child interplay is the experience of "indwelling." The hallmark of this experience is that the child feels like she lives in, and owns, her own body. Stolorow and Atwood (1992) note, "with the achievement of indwelling, the skin becomes the subjective boundary between the self and nonself" (p. 46). Failure to achieve this experience creates a vulnerability to "mind-body disintegration" (e.g., depersonalization, derealization, and disso-ciation). In what follows, I suggest that this failure, and the resultant difficulty in recognizing the boundaries of the self, makes the individual vulnerable to the use of self-mutilation as a means of defining the self at times of threat-ened disorganization. Cutting becomes a means of concretely representing the weak and destructible boundary of the skin.

A sensitive mother anticipates her infant's needs and quickly responds to signs of tension, giving the infant the healthy illusion of omnipotent control over the mother's responses. Winnicott (1971) suggests that the absence of this early experience of control of gratification from the outer world mitigates against a true appreciation and enjoyment of reality. Instead, the infant is forced into a premature experience of disorganizing need with no relief from the external world. This begins to link the experience of longing with terror and psychic catastrophe. The stage is set for reliance on dissociation as relief from the press of an unbearable world as well as unsatisfiable longing.

Christine experienced her mother as incapable of attuned care. She saw her as a dangerous figure who, because of her own depression and alcoholism, preference for boys, and an unmetabolized history of sexual abuse, had little to offer. This view of her mother, and Christine's own reliance on action over words, her pronounced counterdependent stance, and her hatred of reality (as reflected in her reliance on dissociation) point to traumatic early disruption and a consequent failure to achieve a sense of embodiment, with the result that her skin was not the intact, symbolic boundary between herself and the world. The likely misattunement between mother and infant, and the possible use of Christine by her mother as a receptacle for mother's unbearable affect, was represented concretely in a story Christine told of her experience in early childhood.

Like Christine, her mother was one of the middle children in a large fam-ily. At age three, Christine went to live for a period of time with her mother's parents. As a child, Christine's mother had been sexually abused by her fa-ther, and physically abused by her mother. By sending Christine to live with her parents, her mother created the opportunity for Christine to bear what had been unbearable for her. While living in her grandparents' home, Christine reported being molested by her grandfather and beaten by her grandmother. As an adult, in a rare moment of speaking about her own experience, Christine told her mother about this abuse. According to Christine, her mother's response was "I went through it, now you'll have to, too." She was overwhelmed by the undeniable realization that her mother had sent her to her grandparents with knowledge of their abusiveness, thus further concretizing her role as a receptacle for what could not be borne by her mother.

Christine and her family colluded to perpetuate this use of Christine as a receptacle for the family "garbage." Unlike all of her brothers and sisters, Christine never married and never had children. She was, in a metaphorical and concrete sense, "at their disposal." Whenever family members, including her multiple nieces and nephews, needed anything they would turn to her. Time after time, she would allow herself to be exploited, both financially and emotionally, with seeming naiveté. It was not until well into her treatment that she had awareness of her reactive anger. As Modell notes in this volume, "We take for granted the primary metaphor that our body is a container into which we place 'good' substances and from which we expel noxious substances. From this primitive and universal experience, we form the schema that we take into the container what is good and eject what is bad" (p. 4). I believe the relentless experience of being filled with the noxious substances that others could not bear, and having her meager resources plundered, left Christine with the experience that she did not own her "body as container" and reversed the developmental belief that what is inside is "good and containable." For Christine what was inside was foreign, noxious, and damaging.

In her therapy hours, Christine was typically pragmatic, virtually free of affective outbursts, and devoid of metaphoric speech. She spoke of events and behaviors. The creation of a reflective space for exploration of the meaning, or even the context, of her self-mutilation was stymied by the fact that her dissociation left her "clueless." Bodily longings, frustrations, disappointments, and affectively charged identifications and interactions were relegated to her dissociated moments. When dissociated, Christine could approach her femininity through the purchase of dresses, her longings through sexual encounters, and her rage through barroom fights. In the absence of dissociation, she was vigilant about limiting stimulation, lest she be overwhelmed by unnamable tension.

Christine's lack of language for her experience of being used by others, her inability to name and face her own powerful feelings, and her related confusion about the ownership of her body may all have been concretized through her damage to her own skin. Her deep and brutal cutting created on the surface of her body a manifestation of herself as a damaged container. Through her mutilated skin, she presented herself to me and to the world as a body that could not hold its physical or psychological contents. Her self-mutilation communicated the central dilemma of her treatment—her bodily boundary could not keep things in or out.

THE IMPORTANCE OF SKIN

Bick (1968) emphasized the centrality of skin as the earliest and primary site of mother-infant contact. She spoke of skin as the primitive, bodily container of identity. Bick recast Bion's largely psychological process of containment into a physical containment, created by skin-to-skin contact, and resulting in the infant attaining her first feeling of existence. "The skin, in a sense, is the site of the self" (Hinshelwood 1997, 310). If psychological containment fails, the individual is prone to developing a false self (Shapiro 1982; Sacksteder 1989). If the containing function of the skin is not experienced, the self is prone to fragmentation and dissolution.

Christine came to her first hour wearing a man's tee shirt and jeans, her typical garb throughout our work together. She looked tough, without a hint of femininity. Every bit of skin that could be seen, including her face, was covered with scars from her self-inflicted injuries. On this first day, the caption on her shirt read "Stress: The Confusion Created When the Mind Must Override the Body's Basic Desire to Choke the Living Crap Out of Some Idiot Who Desperately Deserves It!" She had been involved in several barroom fights prior to admission, and, on one occasion, returned to the hospital with a black eye and split lip but without memory of what had happened. Frequently she spoke with me about her intention to "beat the crap" out of anyone who threatened her.

Christine's contrasting presentation of a vulnerable body covered with wounds and her counterdependent, aggressive stance illustrates vividly Bick's notion of a defensive "second skin," where early dependency needs are replaced by pseudo-independence and the "inappropriate use of certain mental functions . . . (to create) a substitute for this skin container function" (Bick 1968, 484). As was the case with Christine, this second skin is often in the form of a physical or verbal "muscularity." Her bravado and physical threats fended off those who might enter the space left unprotected by her damaged self and skin. I regularly felt jarred by her tone and language, perhaps recreating in me her own early experience of misattuned touch and voice.

Like the infants in Bick's description, Christine had a "profound lack of integration of body, posture, motility, and (the) corresponding function of the mind, particularly communication" (p. 486). She could not hold all of her parts together, and her chronic dissociation was the most striking manifestation of this lack of integration. Christine's longings, as expressed through the dissociated purchase of comforts for her home and feminine clothing (which she experienced as alien and gave away once the dissociation passed), and through sexual liaisons, were profoundly disconnected from her awareness. Consciously, she spoke with pride of not needing anyone and "wanting to keep it that way," as well as her hatred of being physically touched. She noted with disdain that a previous therapist had recommended massage as a way of getting more "in touch with her body." Christine's response was "I don't want no stranger touching my body."

SELF-SOOTHING AND THE USE OF
PRIMITIVE "TRANSITIONAL OBJECTS"

In the situation of "good enough mothering" (Winnicott 1960) there exists a mother-infant unit in which the infant's biological rhythms are felt and responded to and the infant is protected from over- or under-stimulation. Through this experience, the infant gains a kind of security that leads to a basic sense that existence will continue—to use Winnicott's (1960) term, a sense of "going on being." Infants who achieve this fundamental security and continue to receive adequate caretaking gradually take over these functions, allowing the recognition that self and other are separate. Transitional objects that represent both the infant's longed-for oneness with the mother and the dawning recognition of external reality provide visual, tactile, and olfactory soothing, both connected with and separate from the mother.

What then of the infants who do not reliably experience gratification and soothing at the time of their need and therefore do not develop the sense of "going on being"? These infants, instead of moving on to face separateness, are preoccupied with maintaining basic homeostasis. Patients with such a history in infancy may have a terror of dissolution for which there are few forms of comfort. Bick (1968) suggests that "the need for a containing object would seem in the infantile unintegrated state to produce a frantic search for an object—a light, a voice, a smell or other sensual object—which can hold the attention and thereby be experienced, momentarily at least, as holding the parts of the personality together" (p. 484). These infants lean on soothing, repeated behavior patterns, or sensation-dominated experiences, akin to transitional objects but at a more concrete, primitive level (Tustin 1980; Gaddini 1969). Unlike the more developed and more symbolic transitional objects that protect against the anxiety of the loss of the just-barely-perceived other, these more primitive "objects" protect against the anxiety of self-fragmentation and the loss of the self.

Through her work with autistic children, Tustin (1980) became aware of particular maneuvers that these children use to soothe themselves, holding at bay the underlying catastrophic anxiety of dissolution. She suggests that similar mechanisms operate in those adults who, at their core, fear self-fragmentation. These mechanisms include repeated patterns of behavior that create sensations on the surface of the skin that simultaneously provide an early autoerotic substitute for the experience of maternal comfort, soothing, and holding, and help delineate a defensive shield of separateness and impenetrability (Ogden 1989). Like the organizing experience of fixing on a light, smell, or voice, as referred to by Bick, autistic objects both orient and protect. Ogden notes, "An autistic object is a safety generating sensory impression . . . that defines, delineates and protects one's otherwise exposed and vulnerable surface" (p. 56). He suggests that repeated mental operations, compulsive exercise, and ritualized eating may represent such autistic defenses.

In the treatment hours, typically in the context of a moment of understanding between us, Christine would find herself counting backwards from one hundred. She stated that her skin would begin to tingle and her heart pound. In the face of her momentary softening, she would rely on this operation to recreate her hardened shell. Christine used counting as an autistic object that reduced her inner tension and created a protective shield between us. Similarly, she reported that alone in her room at night she would have "visual hallucinations" of benign, faceless people. Rather than venture out into the unpredictable and uncontrollable milieu, she comforted herself in isolation.

I would suggest that Christine's cutting was both an autistic defense and a manifestation of her body as a damaged container. Christine had achieved neither a sense of "indwelling" nor the basic security of "going on being." Christine's repetitive self-mutilation served the dual function of staving off dissolution and expressing her terrifying longings for sensual contact. Her skin coming into contact with the blade would bring Christine back to the recognition of her need for her crusty shell. She would stop dissociating and leave behind her longings. Her damaged skin, however, became the site of repeated physical ministering. While being treated as an outpatient, she would travel from emergency room to emergency room, seeking out caregivers to suture her wounds who did not know of the repetitive nature of her behavior and who therefore were less likely to be angered by her presentation. She repeatedly sought skin-to-skin contact, accompanied by soothing, not harsh voices. This contact, however, was not at the level of self-other interaction; it served as an autistic defensive maneuver that helped her to feel calmed. In a sense she found "her continuity of being in the continuity of doing" (Brusset

1977 as reported in Jeammet 1988). I believe that this process contained a deeply buried hopefulness. The repeated contact with medical personnel, through which her aggression could be metabolized rather than reprojected into her, evoked in her the possibility of reexperiencing her dependency and ultimately facing her separateness. The repeated process of cutting and watching her skin heal may have also reflected an omnipotent fantasy of self-repair and self-regeneration. In a sense, her healing was a repeated, hopeful, albeit relatively isolated, attempt to reclaim the capacity to develop a containing body.

TREATMENT IMPLICATIONS

The notion of Christine as a container, damaged by the projection into her of unbearable aspects of her mother's and other family members' experiences, had implications for the transference and countertransference and for an approach to treatment, particularly in the earliest phases. Christine's experience of being "asked" to bear more than she could tolerate was repeated in her early interactions with me. I felt filled with feelings that she did not experience. Her affectively bland descriptions of her sliced skin, her perforated cheek, the smell of burned flesh, her ten—twenty—fifty sutures, all left me feeling sickened by her words and "done to" by her process. Through our interchanges, she induced in me the experience of being filled with an unnamable horror and sadness. Tacitly, she asked me to resonate with her horror. My task was both to attempt to offer her manageable reflections of what she was unable to verbalize and to understand the ways in which I would inevitably fail her in this process

Initially, in what I later came to see as premature interpretations, I spoke with her about the seemingly tortured and torturing dance in which we were engaged, in which she was numb and I was filled with excruciating distress. She would respond to such comments with bland assent, but the deadness in her face indicated that I had lost her. Through interpreting the sadomasochistic dynamic implicit in our process, I had distorted her felt experience as I linked it to mine. I came to see that I had to use restraint in disclosing what she stirred in me so as not to destructively reenact the early dynamic of turning her into a receptacle for feelings that were difficult for me to contain. Although there was significant aggression in her interactions with me, it became clear that we, as an early dyad, were not yet ready to speak of it. The dance that could be spoken of was not the sadomasochistic one, but instead the longed-for dance of mutual cuing between mother and infant—a dance in which both participants are learners.

Christine loved to drive. One day she spoke of driving close to one hundred miles an hour on the local interstate, blasting her radio. I noticed that as she described her actions I was "white knuckled," gripping the arms of my chair as though I too were being hurled through space. Containing my wish both to lecture her about the danger of such behavior and to interpret the hostility and grandiosity involved in taking me on this wild ride, I noted her apparent sense of contentment. We spoke of the lengths to which she had to go—being encased by steel, moving at one hundred miles per hour, blocking out internal stimuli through the blaring sound—in order to protect herself from intrusions. She spoke of the unequalled safety she felt in this context. She was teaching me about the need to stay close to her experience. As we discussed her need to be impenetrable, we were beginning to discover a context in which she could allow me to contact her.

Christine's deep ambivalence about making contact was prominent in the transference. Negotiations and actions around the framework of treatment are a symbolic kind of touching between therapist and patient. Christine was exquisitely sensitive to my planned absences, not speaking about her experience but demonstrating her response through an escalation in dissociation and cutting. My absences were an affront to her grandiosity—she could not control me and, despite my knowledge of her need, I left. One day, I arranged with her to move our appointment back ten minutes because I was worried I might not make it back in time from an off-grounds appointment. Christine came at our newly arranged time and was blustery throughout the session, complaining about what she saw as unfair treatment the night before by the nursing staff. At twenty minutes past the hour, our normal ending time, Christine got up to leave. I was startled. Her assumption was that my negotiating with her to begin ten minutes *later* meant that I was giving her ten minutes *less*. The unfair treatment that she was speaking of was mine. My attempt to place her discussion within the context of our hour led initially to a softening and flicker of interest. But, just as quickly, her skin began to itch and her eyes started to dart about the room, the somatic symptoms that typically preceded dissociative episodes. My interpretation both caught her attention and called for a simultaneous defensive retreat because implicit in it was an acknowledgment of our connection.

DISCUSSION

Like many patients who self-mutilate, this patient was psychologically abandoned through physical and sexual abuse. Her early and repeated psychological experience of being used as a receptacle for others' projections created a vulnerability that led her experience of physical and sexual abuse to be devastating. For patients who do not experience ownership of their bodies, repeated physical, sexual, and psychological intrusions are catastrophic, reinforcing the need for autistic isolation. This patient's significant history of trauma suggests that sadomasochistic themes and the almost caricatured delineations of victim and perpetrator would ultimately need to be addressed in treatment. However, these dynamics could not be approached until at least a rudimentary ability to contain was achieved.

Locating the severe self-mutilation and chaotic symptom picture of this patient within the early symbiotic phase of development helped to create a containing and orienting frame of reference for our work. The focus on the dynamics of early infancy was not a preconception on my part, but rather emerged as Christine gradually helped me to find her. Our increasing effort to formulate the dynamics of containment in the early mother-infant relationship (and in the therapist-patient dyad), to articulate her experience of her skin, and to describe her use of autistic defenses suggested potential meaning for what might otherwise have seemed an unrelated catalogue of psychotic symptoms. Her effort to grapple somatically with the intrusive, betraying other (the mother of childhood, the adult abusers and exploiters, and myself in the transference) who invaded both physically and psychologically led to dissociation and somatic responses, fueled by uncontained, chaotic and formless internal experience. This formulation helped to protect me, as a therapist, from what might otherwise have been an overwhelming assault by the patient's unrelenting symptoms and the grief of such profound human tragedy. The structure provided by this developmental perspective provided a containing framework within which the two of us could begin to develop a shared language for otherwise unbearable experience.

Not all patients who self-mutilate have experienced the almost unthinkable extremes of misattunement, exploitation, and projection that Christine reported. Some patients who cut do not report a history of sexual or physical abuse, or do not find such abuse utterly catastrophic. They are able to speak vividly of the psychological impact of cutting, the experience of their bodies, and of their relationships. For these patients, self-mutilation may not represent an underlying failure to achieve the experience of embodiment but instead may be a regression to a symbolic communication about threats to embodiment posed by intrapsychic and interpersonal dynamics.

Many patients who cut speak about the experience of partial dissociation— of bodily and affective numbness. The sight of their own blood is often the sensual experience that recreates a sense of "indwelling"; with the sight of blood, bodily sensations return along with affects and the experience of having a body. I would suggest that here, too, conceptualizing the individual as a receptacle for unmetabolized experience from the interpersonal field can provide guideposts for treatment. Beginning to put into language the experience of the self-as-container, prone to accepting noxious, destructive projections, can allow the individual to contemplate the creation or healing of a skin that contains the self and keeps out what is foreign.

I thank Drs. Rita Frankiel, John Muller, Yasmin Roberts, Edward Shapiro, and Jane Tillman for their helpful comments.

REFERENCES

Bick, E. (1968). The experience of the skin in early object relations. *International Journal of Psychoanalysis*, 49, 484–86.

Bion, W. R. (1962). *Learning from Experience*. London, Heinemann.

Brusset, R. (1977). *L'assiette et le Miroir*. Private ed. Paris.

Fonagy, P. and Target, M. (2000). Playing with reality III: The persistence of dual psychic reality in borderline patients. *International Journal of Psychoanalysis*, 81, 853.

Gaddini, E. (1969). On imitation. *International Journal of Psychoanalysis*, 50, 475–84.

Hinshelwood, R. D. (1997). Catastrophe, objects and representation: Three levels of interpretation. *British Journal of Psychotherapy*, 13(3), 307–17.

Jeammet, P. (1988). Discussion of Regina Casper's presentation: Psychodynamic psychotherapy in acute anorexia nervosa. In A. Esman, ed., *International Annals of Adolescent Psychiatry* (pp. 225–38). Chicago: University of Chicago Press.

Ogden, T. (1989). *The Primitive Edge of Experience*. Northvale, NJ: Jason Aronson.

Sacksteder. J. (1989). Psychosomatic dissociation and false self-development in anorexia nervosa. In M. Fromm and B. Smith, eds., *The Facilitating Environment: Clinical Applications of Winnicott's Theory* (pp. 365–93). Madison, CT: International Universities Press.

Shapiro, E. R. (1982). On curiosity: Intrapsychic and interpersonal boundary formation in family life. *International Journal of Family Psychiatry*, 3, 69–89.

Stolorow, R. and Atwood, G. (1992). *The Contexts of Being: The Intersubjective Foundations of Psychological Life*. Hillsdale, NJ: The Analytic Press.

Tillman, J. G. (1999). Erotized transference and self-mutilation. *Psychoanalytic Review*, 86(5), 709–20.

Tustin, F. (1980). Autistic objects. *International Review of Psycho-Analysis*, 7, 27–39.

Winnicott, D. (1960). The theory of the parent-infant relationship. *International Journal of Psychoanalysis*, 41, 585–95.

—— (1971). Mirror-role of mother and family in child development. In *Playing and Reality* (pp. 111–18). New York: Basic Books.

Woodruff, M.E. (1999). Flesh made word: Cutting back to the mother. *Psychoanalytic Review*, 86(5), 701–8.

Chapter Seven

The Transition from Bodies to Words: A Clinical Illustration

M. Gerard Fromm, Ph.D.

INTRODUCTION

In his discussion of psychosomatic symptoms, Adam Phillips writes, "It is the psychoanalytic wish that words can lure bodies back to words . . . It is always worth wondering . . . what picture we have of what words can do to someone's body, of how they work inside him. And conversely, what bodily symptoms . . . can do to our own words and bodies" (Phillips 1996, 36). Nina Coltart makes a similar point: "We could say that a psychosomatic symptom represents that which is determined to remain unconscious, or unknowable, but which at the same time has actually made itself conscious in a very heavy disguise; it is speakable about only in a dense and enigmatic code . . . How do we build a bridge which *really holds* over the secret area of the body-mind divide? Can the unthinkable become thinkable?" (Coltart 1986, 198).

The clinical situation to be described approaches these questions through the concepts of transitional phenomena and enactment. The patient's present-ing symptoms focused around serious substance abuse and depression. His substance abuse began as a way of dealing with migraine headaches, among other bodily symptoms of extreme tension, which itself was the result of se-vere anxiety in his vocational and social life. I hope to illustrate a number of clinical points, including (1) the way in which the constellation of feelings around the patient's drug use replicated in a very specific way, and yet also displaced and disguised, the constellation of feelings around childhood sex-ual abuse, experiences for which the patient had for many years been amnes-tic; (2) the essentially corrupt relation between his drug cravings and his psy-chosomatic symptoms; and (3) most importantly, the way in which the act of substance abuse assumed powerful transference meaning, which placed the drug's function of affect regulation in a matrix of early object relationships.

CLINICAL MATERIAL

The patient, an appealing but inhibited young man, came to a residential treatment center following his third inpatient hospitalization for substance abuse treatment. The treatment setting is a small, open, and voluntary hospital-based therapeutic community in which patients are seen in four-times-weekly psychoanalytic psychotherapy. This patient's promising career had collapsed because of his addiction to opiate medication, drugs that had actually become his secret solution to the intense anxiety, desperation to please and frantic overinvestment he experienced in his work life. While this level of driven devotion had earned him promotions and the regard of his boss, it was unsustainable, and this registered in the patient's body. Simultaneously, his first serious love relationship was also collapsing under the strain of his effort to please his partner, his jealous certainty that he could not, and his intense conflict about his own sexual pleasure.

The patient arrived for treatment very depressed, mildly disorganized, full of insecurity and self-criticism, and suffering a number of bodily symptoms of extreme tension: neck and jaw stiffness, backache, stomach upset and recurrent migraine headaches. For his headaches, which the patient reported and the residential staff observed to be unbearably painful, the internist, an experienced doctor who is generally very conservative, continued the patient's prescription of potentially addictive painkilling medication—to be used in limited doses for short periods of time after other remedies for his migraines had been tried. The patient formed a good therapeutic alliance, and, over the course of time, he began to recognize that the unbearable anxiety that had led to his addiction had as its background two important contexts: the death of his mother several years before, and periodic sexual abuse by a camp counselor during his latency years. The patient reported, quite believably, that he had repressed the memory of these summer sexual events throughout his rather withdrawn adolescence, but that his beginning to date in college had brought them back with disorganizing clarity.

Over time, as this not particularly psychologically minded but hardworking patient put his experiences of addiction and of sexuality into words, and especially as he noticed his associations moving from one to the other recurrently, it began to seem clear that a powerful unconscious relationship existed between them. Indeed, it came to seem that the intrapsychic scenario around drug abuse functioned both to hide but also to represent in disguised form the specific constellation of repressed feelings and memories relating to sexual abuse. Slowly the patient developed the ability to articulate these feelings, first in relation to drugs and then cautiously in relation to the childhood sexual scenario. He described feelings of emptiness and of being left out, which led to a need for something to make him feel better. The possibility of having this need met by a drug or by the camp counselor's attention brought excitement, craving, and a sense of compulsion. It also brought fear, since he recognized that something forbidden was happening. Both situations also made him feel special and pleasurably powerful. He felt the power to get something he wanted, to have a secret, and to get away with something. Afterward, he felt ashamed, isolated, damaged and in need of punishment. As though to cement the connection between drug abuse and sexuality, the patient reported that he had taken to using drugs to numb current sexual excitement with his girlfriend, because he felt paralyzed with her and could not relax into allowing himself sexual pleasure as an adult.

This powerfully convincing phase of analytic work, which brought considerable relief to the patient's chronic anxiety and bodily tension, came fully alive in relation to the patient's headaches and his use of prescribed but potentially addictive medication to treat them. As the feelings described above became increasingly conscious in the patient's daily life, he came to realize the corrupt relationship between his headaches and his drug cravings. In essence, he found that he no longer needed the medication for his headaches; but he needed his headaches for the medication. His headaches were the outcome of the burgeoning tension of his craving for medication. He found himself making efforts to control the craving by not telling himself about this intense feeling, while he was also simultaneously calculating the risks and rationalizing the pleasures associated with getting what he wanted. Eventually, a headache would actually develop, a pain that truly "needed" but also paid off the guilt for getting the forbidden substance.

Erikson titled one of his collections of essays *Insight and Responsibility* (1964). My patient had come to realize with conviction that he was continuing his addiction (and his psychosomatic symptoms) with *our* [therapist and physician] medication. What was his responsibility now to his treatment and to the prescriber? And, given that I had referred him to this physician, what was mine? The patient did not initiate a reduction of painkilling medication; instead he played out the status quo with ever more clarity about what he was doing. In the transference-countertransference situation, I then began to feel like the illicit partner of a childhood scenario. Yet, I felt it important not to react from a superego position to the collusive aspects of this situation. The patient had made a critical discovery in the midst of our enacting the trouble (enacting it by my providing the forbidden substance in the first place and then by my silence toward the prescribing physician). I felt I had to tolerate this collusion for the time being, so that from inside the transference situation, we might find the words to describe the dilemma and its potential meanings.

If the psychotherapy could function as a holding environment for this situation, the patient might take a lead in finding our way out of it.

Working through this dilemma began with recognition of the "panic" the patient felt at the thought that his medications would be "taken away" if he spoke honestly to the prescriber. This did not come across as an exaggeration; it was as though some basic life-sustaining connection would be severed. I put this highly charged metaphor back to the patient, with the half-formed fantasy in my mind that he clung to his medications the way a young child clings to a security blanket. To my surprise, this psychologically unsophisticated patient associated it to giving up breast-feeding as an infant. He did indeed discover transitional objects at that time to which he became powerfully, if mournfully, attached. Most of all, he recalled an ongoing unsatisfied craving for his mother during his early childhood, as well as how uncomprehending his mother seemed to be about this. Over time it seemed that this youngest child and only son was looking to his mother for protection from the ongoing resentment and envy of his physically aggressive older sister. His mother, however, who had lost her own mother early in her life, was oriented more toward pleasing her daughter than setting limits for her. Given the father's prolonged absences because of his career, the patient submerged his anger in a defensive and unworkable identification with his mother, which nevertheless left him quite vulnerable to the attention of the camp counselor, and later to the demands of his boss.

Suddenly, the early childhood sexuality for which the patient felt so guilty seemed to have as its background painful experiences of oral longing and problematic weaning. With this new perspective, the patient could begin to feel empathy for himself. He recalled one particularly disturbing scene of early childhood in which his mother could not understand why her son was so upset, nor could he explain it. This scene seemed prototypic of the "taken away" feeling in the sense that the patient could not reach his mother communicatively, and she lost patience with him.

As all of this took shape, I brought the patient back to our present dilemma, and I suggested to him that rather than telling the prescriber he no longer needed his medication in the amount that was available, he take it upon himself to use as little as possible, eventually stopping it altogether. In this way, medication would not be taken away; rather he would be letting it go. This shift of the locus of authority placed the medications into, or perhaps more accurately, recognized the medications as already in a transitional space (Winnicott 1958a) over which the patient has rights. In a sense, I joined the patient's solution to the problems associated with his unconscious needs for both oral nurturance and for survivable weaning. The patient took my recommendation fully, used considerably less of an already relatively small amount of medication, and had fewer headaches in the process. He felt much more in charge of himself and more deeply involved in his therapy.

However, there was a crucial next phase to this problem. After a number of months of very little use of his painkilling medication, the patient made no move in the direction of formally discontinuing it. Instead, he occasionally used it as an antianxiety agent, rather than as a treatment for migraines. Once more, I had the gathering feeling of being his illicit partner as well as the idealized, but in some ways corrupt, father who paid for his absences by allowing his son to do whatever he wanted. Interpretation of this transference-countertransference dynamic, however, did not really take hold until, in Winnicott's (1969) language about a child's coming to be able to "use the object," I moved to place myself outside the patient's projections and inside my connection to other treatment personnel. In a different language, the patient's transitional relationship to his medication drifted contentedly into a low-key omnipotence in relation to it and to me, and I found myself feeling an approaching limit inside myself.

Eventually, I confronted the patient. I reviewed with him very specifically what he and I had come to learn about the meaning of these medications genetically, and what their consequences were now to his self-esteem and psychosomatic inclination. I reviewed his experience over some months of his doing almost completely without the medications and his own recognition of the importance of moving to a forthright and trusting relationship with all of us to provide what might be needed should he suffer a recurrence of symptoms in the future. And yet, he had not taken the necessary next step, and I pressed him to examine why.

The patient experienced this as a serious confrontation and rather quickly found himself with an answer: because then I would experience him without drugs (and without the refuge of their imagined availability); I would see his ugly side, including the side of him that would want more from me than I could give, and I would not be able to stand it.

In a sense this was a serious confrontation in return that opened up the deeper transference feelings toward the mother who could not stand his childhood demands, and to the family culture of buying off ugly needs with pacifying gifts, keeping up appearances in the process. In the transference, my allowing these medications was my pacifying gift. Aggression, and the potential for surviving it (Winnicott 1969), had now entered the transference relationship, and the patient could now take the risk of leaving both of us unprotected by fully terminating his prescription, which he did.

Occasional incidents of drug use (the patient was very skilled at acquiring the drugs he needed) occurred thereafter, usually on trips home, each of which led to microanalysis and deeper insight. I maintained a stance of benign neutrality about the state of our alliance around his acquiring further drugs: I neither believed him nor disbelieved him about his being drug-free. Later in his treatment, he admitted his periodic dishonesty with me during this post-prescription phase, which had to do once again with protection of him and me. He thought that I might take his few brief, self-managed relapses as a sign that he needed a drug treatment program, and "if you had sent me away, I would have wanted to kill you."

DISCUSSION

As noted earlier, Coltart (1986, 198) hopes for a "bridge" that "really holds" over "the body-mind divide." The idea of a "divide" describes a split between soma and psyche. It calls to mind Winnicott's (1965, 148) description of the gap between the true and false self. The former is primarily bodily experience, "no more than . . . the details of the experience of aliveness," ordinary, and indeed at the beginning, autonomic. Conversely, the "false self" represents a hypertrophied and dissociative form of psychic adaptation, sometimes localized in the mind. A "bridge" also suggests both the concept of instinct, which Freud (1915/1957, 122) tells us exists "on the frontier" between body and mind, and the concept of transitional space (Winnicott 1958a). The latter defines a form of psychic bridge-building insofar as it describes the restorative experience of enough similarity within difference, or proximity within separateness, such that the self as agent can join the other.

Both concepts seem relevant to the work with this patient. My initial stance regarding his medications could be viewed as instinctual enactment in "that secret area," as Coltart puts it, of body-mind divide. I had allowed the internist to prescribe addicting medication from the beginning, then did not initiate discontinuation of it once its meaning had become clear and the use of it unnecessary. Had it not been for our long-standing and trusting working relationship, the internist and I could easily have seemed, or actually become, like the patient's parents, absent to each other and absent as a holding pair for the patient. For me, it was essential that I keep both the internist and the patient in mind as I found myself situated within the enactment. In this space, what was discovered was the transitional function of the medications. For this patient, the medications were not simply about restoring security through the illusion of being able to omnipotently have whatever he needed. They were also the protosymbolic bridge across the early gap between the bodily distress of the needy child and the failures of comprehension or reflective functioning within his mother. In the transference, they represented his defense against depending fully on me and against the rage he would have felt had I failed him in a similar way.

The patient used this phase of what might be called transitional enactment, that is, enactment in the service of bridging a critical gap between self and other, to wean himself from the medications, but even more to rediscover the lost child within what he had taken to be only the bad child. My recommendation to him about his taking it upon himself to reduce and discontinue his medications functioned technically as an interpretation of the transitional meaning of the medications, and conveyed to him that I understood something he felt his mother had not. In this context, he could take more risks.

This phase of enactment, however, eventually had to come to a complete end if a genuine and durable level of dependency on me and on those who helped me was to be achieved. This latter move meant the patient forfeiting the protections of transitional space, giving up his medications altogether, and, risking a directness of aggression between us. As we worked through and lived through this successfully, the patient was able to take up a job, working hard but without feeling driven to please, and to his great amazement, he began a sexually fulfilling love relationship with a woman.

Analytic literature on substance abuse rightly highlights the vicissitudes of affect regulation (Khantzian 1999). What I hope to have illustrated in this focused clinical contribution is the way in which the constellation of feelings and unconscious fantasies in relation to the *act* of substance abuse played out a specific childhood scenario in the transference, in this case related to childhood sexual experience. The anxiety, anger, and guilt related to his sexuality were lodged in my patient's body in the painful psychosomatic tension states that seriously interrupted his functioning. His letting go of his psychosomatic symptoms, his drugs, and transferentially his conflicted claim on his mother came about first through the establishment of a transitional space in which I became his secret, potentially collusive partner.

Within this "secret partner" relationship, as perhaps had also been true with the camp counselor, I carried the condensation of two sets of transference elements. First, like his mother before weaning, I was to continue the supply of love, attention, and holding-in-mind that he felt he so abruptly lost. I was to be the silent, maternal partner of early life, who disappears into the child's illusion that he has rights over this bit of the external world, indeed that he invented it in the first place. But, second, I also felt his longing for his absent father to step into the painful separateness between his mother and him and to mobilize and survive the estranged aggression in that earlier relationship. For all of its seriously damaging effects, the sexuality with the camp counselor represented, from this angle, a push forward in psychosexual development, an effort to find a man who would help him move beyond the maternal relationship, as did the complex collusion around his substance abuse into which he invited me.

The phase of enactment within his psychotherapy was eventually terminated less by interpretation than by my decision, based on my assessment of his developing insight and strengths, to confront this form of relating as a newly evolved resistance. These moments require careful "handling," which is Winnicott's (1958b) word for that early child care process in which the primary caretaker introduces and reintroduces the baby to his or her body through the communicative quality of physical ministrations. There may be a corollary in analysis in which, perhaps especially with psychosomatic patients, our words and voice "handle" the psyche (Sacksteder 1989), bridge the "divide" between physicality and mindfulness, and facilitate the process of bringing "bodies back to words."

On the other hand, "handling" is a maternal function, and as I have noted, my interpretive words with this patient did not truly effect the enactment until I changed my location, so to speak. Perhaps transitional space, which has generative potential, had with this patient settled into a defensive, simply dyadic space, the unintegratable space of a secret gratification. However one thinks of it, the move I needed to make was toward Thirdness (Muller 1996): concretely, toward the third party of the internist; transferentially, toward the third party of the father; and symbolically, toward the social order in which I had my role and my patient might eventually find his. In Winnicott's insight into the use of the object, we also find this crucial opening onto Thirdness. What he most uniquely adds to its understanding is the fact of its developmental discovery through destructiveness and survival.

This destructiveness, quiet though it may have been with my patient, registered in the countertransference and needed to become the basis for nonretaliatory analytic responsiveness from a place outside transitional space. Transitional enactment after a time needed a return action from me, a mobilizing of the growing feeling in my body, in order for words to assume and carry psychic weight. The "bridge" in this clinical situation between soma and psyche was in effect a two-step process, beginning with the establishment of a transitional space and its corollary enactment, and ending with the discovery of workable otherness.

REFERENCES

Coltart, N. (1986). 'Slouching towards Bethlehem' . . . or thinking the unthinkable in psychoanalysis. In G. Kohon, ed., *The British School of Psychoanalysis: The Independent Tradition* (pp. 185–99). New Haven, CT: Yale University Press.

Erikson, E. H. (1964). *Insight and Responsibility*. New York: W.W. Norton & Co.

Freud, S. (1957). Instincts and their vissicitudes. In J. Strachey, ed. and trans., *The Standard Edition of the Complete Psychological Works of Sigmund Freud*, Vol. 4 (pp. 109-40). London: Hogarth Press. (Original work published 1915)

Khantzian, E. (1999). *Treating Addiction as a Human Process*. Northvale, NJ: Jason Aronson.

Muller, J. (1996). *Beyond the Psychoanalytic Dyad*. New York: Routledge.

Phillips, A. (1996). *Terrors and Experts*. Cambridge, MA: Harvard University Press.

Sacksteder, J. (1989). Personalization as an aspect of the process of change in anorexia nervosa. In M. G. Fromm and B. L. Smith, eds., *The Facilitating Environment: Clinical Applications of Winnicott's Theory* (pp. 394–423). Madison, CT: International Universities Press.

Winnicott, D. W. (1958a). Transitional objects and transitional phenomena. In *Through Paediatrics to Psycho-analysis* (pp. 229–42). New York: Basic Books.

———. (1958b). Metapsychological and clinical aspects of regression within the psycho-analytical set-up. In *Through Paediatrics to Psycho-analysis* (pp. 278–94). New York: Basic Books.

———. (1965). Ego distortion in terms of true and false self. In *The Maturational Processes and the Facilitating Environment* (pp. 140–52). New York: International Universities Press.

———. (1969). The use of an object. *International Journal of Psychoanalysis*, 50, 711–16.

Chapter Eight

Perspectives on Embodiment: From Symptom to Enactment and From Enactment to Sexual Misconduct

Eric M. Plakun, M.D.

THE BODY AND THERAPY

Analysts and therapists often work from the position of a mind-brain split, distinguishing "mind work" from the "brain work" of neurologists and from the "brain" work of general psychiatrists. However, recent developments in neuroscience underscore the ways mind and brain represent aspects of an integrated system (Andreasen 1997, Gabbard 2000, 2005). There is a growing body of compelling evidence for the bodily (i.e., neurophysiological or neuroanatomical) impact of psychiatric disorders and psychotherapy (Spiegel et al. 1989; Baxter et al. 1992; Joffe, Segal, and Singer 1996; Bremner et al. 1997; Putnam and Trickett 1997; Thase et al. 1998). It seems timely to review some of the ways bodies are more part of our "mind work" than we sometimes acknowledge.

Despite our history of comfort with a mind-brain split, and despite the infrequency with which we touch our patients and our steady use of words as the means of communication and therapeutic action in analysis or therapy, bodies play an important, though often understated, role in our work. This chapter does not review the neuroscience of therapy and analysis, but addresses certain manifestations of "embodiment" (i.e., making something bodily or corporeal) in our work. For the sake of simplicity the terms analysis and therapy, and analyst and therapist, are used interchangeably to refer to psychoanalytic work, whether formal analysis or psychodynamic psychotherapy.

In training for analysis, as in embryology, it may be said that "ontogeny recapitulates phylogeny." The experience of individual trainees as they enter the field often repeats the progression of theory in the field. The first lessons trainees learn about bodies in analysis often have to do with symptoms and

103

diagnostic nosology. Trainees learn that bodies are important because a psychiatric patient's symptoms may be bodily, as in such Axis I disorders as anorexia nervosa or somatization disorders, or in work with people struggling with the psychological impact of such bodily disorders as cancer, diabetes mellitus or other medical disorders. In these situations we may spend a good deal of time listening to or speaking with our patients about symptoms related to their bodies. In some of these situations we may even build into the framework of the treatment parameters related to the patient's use or abuse of his or her own body, as when we indicate to a patient with anorexia nervosa that the treatment will not continue unless the patient maintains a weight adequate to ensure that a functioning cognitive apparatus is brought to the therapeutic work.

As trainees become more sophisticated, they learn other ways bodies play a role in therapeutic work. They come to understand the ways a patient's disturbed and disturbing life may play out, in repeated bodily action, that which has been repressed from consciousness and is not understood in words (Freud 1914/1958). Here they learn that an element of the work involves helping patients make the unconscious conscious, by putting the choreography of their repeated behavior into words. An example is the borderline patient who cuts. Analytic exploration of the meaning of the cutting, that is, the deciphering of this encoded action of marking the skin, may allow the patient to stop the behavior.

Eventually trainees learn about countertransference, that is, the notion that it is not only the patient's mind that is relevant in therapeutic work, but also the analyst's. If they read Heimann (1950) and Racker (1968), among others, they will learn that Freud's earliest notion of countertransference as the analyst's transference to the patient, has been broadened to include the totality of the analyst's response to the patient, including responses not dictated by the analyst's particular blind spots, areas of conflict or defenses.

If the trainee reads Sandler (1976, 45), he or she will learn that the analyst brings to the session not only "free-floating attention," but also, inevitably and desirably, "free-floating responsiveness" to the patient based on the analyst's own conflicts and character. Among other things, this means that in the countertransference the analyst's mind and body are relevant to the work, not just the patient's.

The therapist's countertransference may include bodily experienced responses to the patient such as boredom or sleepiness, sexual arousal, sadness, anger, aggressive or sadistic impulses, among others. If a trainee has good-enough supervision, he or she will learn that the countertransference may involve feeling in the therapist aspects of the patient's earlier life experience. In supervision a trainee may also learn that there is no reason to suppose these countertransference responses are reliably invisible to the patient. They are likely to have some influence, however subtle, on the therapist's word choice, tone of voice, posture, and/or behavior. In short, the countertransference will be embodied regardless of the level of training and sophistication of the therapist. After all, a training analysis neither can nor should eliminate a therapist's life history, or character, though it will help if it makes him or her more aware of these and more self-reflective about their impact on treatment.

ENACTMENT

As our hypothetical trainee becomes more sophisticated, he or she will realize, perhaps with the help of a supervisor, that countertransferences are subtly acted out in bodily action in spite of the therapist's best efforts to hold to a position of abstinence and technical neutrality, with free-floating attention and free-floating responsiveness. Here the trainee comes to grips with the experience that has made elucidation of the concept of enactment of central importance in our field.

Enactment has been described (Johan 1992, 841) as a pattern of nonverbal interactional behavior between the two parties in a therapeutic situation that involves a shared regression. As with many definitions, this is so condensed as to elude ready comprehension. It is clear enough that the definition refers to behavior rather than thought or affect alone. This suggests enactments are embodiments. Further, the definition makes it clear enactments involve both analyst and patient, who are interacting.

Fully grasping the notion of enactment is facilitated by attending to its link to the notion of projective identification (Shapiro and Carr 1991; Plakun 1998, 1999) and to the way the analyst is an unwitting participant in it. Shapiro and Carr have noted eight components of projective identification (p. 24), including noticing that the analyst has "an attribute that corresponds" to that disavowed and projected by the patient, that the therapist is involved in "an unconscious collusion" with the process that sustains the projection, and that there is a "complementarity of projections—both participants project" aspects of their own life history into the other.

In an earlier publication (Plakun 1999, 286), the components of enactment have been further elaborated as follows:

> One might think of enactment as a multistep process in which, first, there is the usual "reenactment" in the transference relationship of part of the patient's conflicted or traumatic past . . . . However, in an enactment, the patient's associated unconscious self experience is next disavowed and projected into the

therapist . . . . Enactment begins to become a unique concept, though, when the therapist then participates unwittingly by projecting back into the patient reciprocal and complementary unconscious conflicted countertransference material from the therapist's own life history. The therapist unwittingly colludes with the patient in a process of mutual and complementary projective identification organized around significant past events from the lives of *both* participants. Within such an enactment, the therapist is as much a participant as the patient.

Enactments may be conceptualized as occurring when therapists have trouble tolerating the transference offered by the patient, and/or the associated countertransference (Plakun 2001). In such instances the therapist drifts away from a stance of technical neutrality and abstinence, often by unwittingly either refusing or actualizing the transference (Plakun 1999).

One of the things that is potentially worrisome about enactments is the reality that in an enactment the analyst is, at least for a time, lost in the process of repeating something from his or her past, and acting out the countertransference with the patient. This is a risky position to be in, but one that offers opportunity as well as some danger.

The situation is a bit like that in skiing. In the complex interpersonal terrain of therapy, enactments seem as inevitable a part of the work as sliding downhill is on skis. In both situations one is pulled inexorably in a certain direction, either by the unfolding of the transference-countertransference relationship or by gravity. This is neither good nor bad, but part of the experience. A good skier learns the skill of finding and using his or her edges on the slippery slope, allowing control of the fall downhill. Similarly, a good therapist learns there will be enactments. The trick is to find the edge on this slippery slope that allows him or her to stay poised in a position of technical neutrality and abstinence as best one can.

ENACTMENT AS EMBODIMENT

It should be apparent that in such processes an enactment is highly likely to be embodied in some way, however attenuated. In fact, it is often the realization of some manifestation in the body of the analyst that leads to detection of the enactment. Examples illustrating this assertion abound in the analytic literature. Before the term enactment was introduced, Boyer (1979) discussed his treatment of a woman with whom he became sleepy in sessions. His sleepiness led to a chain of associations and to the analysis of a dream that made him aware of the way his countertransference to the patient engaged conflicted issues from his own past. Boyer realized his sleepiness involved "expressing my anger by withdrawal and refusal to recognize her . . . Such knowledge permitted me to regain my objectivity" (p. 361).

Another example is reported by Jacobs (1986). In his work with a young attorney with well-concealed aggression that escaped Jacobs' notice, the author reports he became aware of a vague sense of discomfort with his patient. He decided to attend specifically to his bodily responses to the patient in sessions: "With regularity, I found my heartbeat to be rapid, my mouth dry, and my guts tense and knotted. It became increasingly clear to me that these were signs of concealed anger occurring in response to the covert anger directed at me" (p. 298). Jacobs was able to analyze his own struggle with aggression in the therapy once he became aware of the way the issues in the treatment recapitulated a situation in his own childhood. He was able to use this discovery to recover his analytic position and confront his patient's aggression in their work.

Another seminal example is McLaughlin's (1991) description of an enactment in which he found himself frustrated by an impasse in the work with a patient who seemed impervious to and rejecting of his interpretations. Despite his awareness of frustration, it was not until McLaughlin became aware of the chain of associations and the meaning of his own unwitting embodiment (i.e., action) that he began to unravel the meaning of the enactment. As he reports, "In groping for clues that might open ways to insight, I caught sight of a somewhat unusual mannerism I had drifted into" (p. 606). McLaughlin describes realizing the removal of his bifocals in sessions recreated for him the childhood experience of being "semi-blind." He traces his countertransference musings about his later move into academic and analytic competence once the world was made clearer by corrective lenses. Further, he links these personal recollections to the clinical situation with his patient, and explains how he was able to use these to advantage in ending the impasse in the analytic work.

Through his enactment, McLaughlin gains an understanding of the way his actions represented an unwitting complementary response to the patient based on his own characterologic "heightened sensitivities to extended attack on, or question of, my seeing and understanding" (p. 608). He realized that this bit of characterologic vulnerability was interfering with his ability to remain in a state of technical neutrality and abstinence with his patient.

More recently, Jacobs (2001) published a report of an enactment involving embodiment. Eighteen months into the treatment of a man whose father had died after a neurologic illness that led to a long, slow cognitive decline, the author realized that he was at an impasse with his patient. Jacobs could make sense of what was happening in the treatment when he discovered he had unwittingly worn to a session mismatched clothing put on while dressing in the dark. He then was able to unravel not only his patient's reaction to his error, but its unconscious determinants in the author's struggle with the impact of his own father's recent stroke and cognitive impairment.

ARE ENACTMENTS BAD?

There has been some controversy in the field about how to think of enactments. Some, like Chused (1997), have espoused a view that enactments are undesirable and to be avoided. Others, like Renik (1993), have argued that enactments are inevitable and useful: For example, Renik suggests "it is helpful to see countertransference enactment as the ever-present raw material of productive analytic technique" (p. 153). Not one to shy away from controversy, Renik goes on to hypothesize that "a sequence of corrective emotional experiences based on transference-countertransference enactments forms the substrate of the treatment" (p. 156).

There is a danger of reifying enactments in a way that can be counterproductive. As the saying goes, when one has a new hammer, everything looks like a nail. Wasserman (1999) has noted that the issue is not the inevitability of enactments that is in question, but whether the overzealous welcoming of enactments may lead the analyst to encourage them needlessly and limit the development of regressive transferences. If a therapist repeatedly acts or speaks, and thus enters enactments, rather than accepting the patient's transference projections, the repeated enactments may interfere with the evolution of the desired transference neurosis. Wasserman's caution is worth taking seriously.

How one sees the role and importance of enactment in therapy depends on the writer's theoretical position. However, it is worth noting that some differences in the inevitability and utility of enactments may follow from differences in the severity of pathology of patients treated. Most who write about enactment are analysts treating relatively high functioning outpatients in psychoanalysis or several-times-weekly psychotherapy. One supposes that a number of the published cases may come from training analyses of candidates. I have suggested elsewhere (Plakun 1998) that some patients are particularly prone to enactment. For example, patients who have experienced childhood abuse or sexual trauma may be particularly enactment-prone, perhaps because of the way the power dynamic of treatment inevitably resonates with the power dynamic of their past abuse. Enactment-prone patients also include those who struggle with severe character pathology as evidenced by marked identity diffusion, major problems with self-esteem and affect regulation, major impairment in interpersonal and occupational functioning, and symptomatic presentations that include self-mutilation and/or need for hospitalization. These patients, frequently diagnosed as "borderline," often make prominent use of splitting, projective identification, and other primitive defenses, and push therapists to the "borderline" of their therapeutic skill (Fromm 1995). Their treatments often become chronic crisis management.

These borderline patients have a reputation for being difficult to treat and for finding and zeroing in on a therapist's areas of character vulnerability. Their preverbal, pre-Oedipal areas of conflict engage a therapist's free-floating responsiveness in a way that pulls for enactment in the countertransference. Treatment of these sicker patients often means the therapeutic pair is never far from enactment. In some instances, these patients require residential treatment.

In residential facilities, the opportunity for an immersion in treatment, the reliance on a dynamic formulation to integrate all aspects of the treatment including therapy, nursing work, milieu treatment, family and substance abuse work, and psychopharmacology, and the ready availability of consultation, supervision, and case review, provide an environment that maximizes the opportunity to use enactments to deepen and advance treatment (Belnap, Iscan, and Plakun 2004). I would propose that for this group of seriously disturbed patients, Renik's (1993) suggestion that enactments are the central substrate of the treatment is often quite literally true.

THE USE OF ENACTMENTS

It is worth wondering what we might like our hypothetical trainee to learn about using enactments. I suggest there are three components to using enactments in therapeutic work that are worth teaching to trainees: detection, analysis in a state of forbearance, and utilization.

With respect to detection, it is apparent that an enactment can be of no use, and may lead to harm, if the analyst remains unaware of it. The analyst's self-attunement allows enactments to be noticed, including in his or her body. The examples cited above contain references to the analyst becoming aware that something unusual was happening involving the analyst's body. There are a myriad of ways an analyst may become aware something is wrong, including an awareness of sleepiness or sexual arousal or irritation with a patient, or anxiety or a sense of bewilderment. The analyst trusts this sense and uses it to become curious about what this experience may mean for him or herself personally and in the therapeutic work. The analyst considers the possibility of an enactment, and begins a search for clues about whether one may be unfolding.

This begins the process of analysis of the enactment, again illustrated in the cases above. The analysis of an enactment is best conducted in a state of forbearance, by which I mean getting hold of and stopping the acting out in the countertransference rather than simply continuing it or reporting it to the patient. One needs time to think and to follow one's associations. This part of the analysis of an enactment is performed in a way that observes the therapeutic dyad as if from the outside, that is, from a transdyadic perspective on the dyad.

Successful analysis of an enactment depends on the therapist's self-knowledge, free-floating attention and free-floating responsiveness. One reason a training analysis or therapeutic experience and supervision are so valuable is because they maximize the chance for the therapist to succeed in the analysis of enactments. Sometimes the therapist is able to complete the analysis of an enactment alone, but often it is necessary to seek supervision or consult with colleagues to concretize the transdyadic perspective. An analyst who becomes certain that he or she has all the self-reflective capacity needed to analyze enactments from an outside perspective entirely on his or her own may be especially vulnerable to becoming lost in the dyad and to countertransference acting out.

Sometimes the therapist turns judiciously to the patient for help with analyzing an enactment. For example, a therapist whose patient complained that the therapist was regularly coming late to sessions asked the patient what she made of this. The therapist was able to use the patient's association that it meant she didn't care about her patient any more to realize that she had been preoccupied with her recent pregnancy, and was struggling with when and how to tell her patients, and with the question of how to find time to be a mother while continuing her professional work.

Once an enactment has been analyzed, utilization of what has been learned in the analysis follows. The specific way it is utilized may vary widely. It may be an interpretation or other action in the therapy, as with Jacobs' (1986) confrontation of his patient's aggression, or an apology if the enactment has involved the therapist injuring the patient with a sadistic remark or condescending tone. The utilization of what has been learned may be a new way of looking at things or recovery of an abstinent and technically neutral stance, as was the case with McLaughlin's (1991) report of an enactment. In any event, the utilization of learning should represent movement back toward traditional therapeutic work. If the utilization of what has been learned is a move in the direction of increased personal self-disclosure or extratherapeutic contact with the patient, there is reason for concern.

Analysts who have successfully followed this sequence of detecting an unwitting enactment, analyzing its meaning from a transdyadic perspective while in a state of forbearance, and utilizing what has been learned, have reported in the literature that impasses have been resolved or therapeutic work deepened.

ENACTMENT AND SEXUAL MISCONDUCT

Problems may arise when one or more of the above components for making use of an enactment do not occur. If an enactment is undetected, an opportunity to deepen the work or resolve an impasse may be missed. The same may be the result if an enactment is detected, but the analysis of its meaning or its utilization are inadequate. The continuation of a treatment in the midst of an enactment that is undetected, unanalyzed and/or not utilized may be problematic. The consequences may range from prolonged impasse and a missed opportunity to deepen the work, to premature termination in a state of impasse, to more ominous developments, particularly when there is a progressive embodiment of an undetected, unanalyzed enactment, as in many cases of therapist sexual misconduct.

Enactments are not simply a royal road to deepening analytic work, but also an area of potential risk, given that they represent acting out of the countertransference to some degree. What holds the therapist in role in an enactment? Renik (1993) has spoken of analytic conscience as a component of this. Our analytic superego constrains us from the active embodiment of every impulse that emerges within us. Renik suggests good analytic technique arises out of the interplay between countertransference and analytic conscience. When, for example, an analyst finds him or herself sexually aroused by a patient, he or she does two things. Analytic conscience leads the analyst to forebear further embodying the impulse or desire, while the analyst engages in reflection on the meaning of the countertransference. Is it related to something external to the therapy with which the analyst is struggling? Is the therapist experiencing something being projected into him or her by the patient? Is the patient behaving overtly in some way that invites this response? If so, is this the kind of response any human being would have to this kind of overture from the patient, or is it in some way unique to a vulnerability, blind spot or conflict in the analyst? As Renik notes, senior analysts are notable not necessarily for the infrequency with which they have countertransference responses or enter enactments, but rather for the comfort with which they have learned to accept the inevitability of countertransference and enactments and the sensitivity and skill with which they use them to deepen and further therapeutic work. As Renik also notes, in almost every instance the analyst enacts the countertransference to some degree before he or she is fully able to understand and decipher it.

Analytic conscience is a useful and comforting notion, but it does not go far enough to explain what restrains an analyst from simply and freely embodying his or her desires. We are all too familiar with instances of senior, and presumably quite skilled, analysts who fail to restrain themselves from crossing sexual boundaries with patients. Is it really adequate to suggest that these analysts have been practicing without an analytic conscience up to the point of the transgression, or that they have always had serious analytic conscience lacunae? This might be a comforting thought, since it allows us to view these analysts as different from us, but it may give us a false sense of security. Further, as illustrated below, it does not adequately fit the available data about what happens in sexual misconduct.

Glen Gabbard (1994, 2003), Gartrell et al. (1986), and Andrea Celenza (1998) have studied therapists who had engaged in sexual misconduct with patients. Gabbard (1994) finds four categories of therapists who commit sexual misconduct: (1) those with psychotic disorders; (2) those who manifest predatory psychopathy in their disregard for their own behavior and lack of empathy for their victims; (3) those suffering from "lovesickness"; and (4) those he sees as fundamentally masochistic and self-destructive. Citing the work of Gartrell et al. (1986), Gabbard notes that 65 percent of therapists who engaged in sexual misconduct with patients, by far the majority, fit his "lovesickness" category. Those therapists who are described as "lovesick" by Gabbard have fallen in love with their patients. In many and perhaps most of these instances, "lovesickness" probably represents an enactment. In fact, Gabbard notes the importance of enactment in cases of therapist sexual misconduct.

In a more recent paper, Gabbard (2003) reports on a sexual boundary violation by "Dr. N," a psychoanalyst who became lost in an enactment in his work with a suicidal patient. Gabbard explores specific mechanisms of enactment that may unfold in the course of work with seriously suicidal patients. These include what he calls disidentification with the aggressor, failure of mentalization, collapse of the analytic play space, reactions to loss in the analyst's personal life, omnipotence, envy of the patient and masochistic surrender.

Celenza (1998) has completed an in-depth study of seventeen therapists involved in sexual misconduct, including interviews with and test batteries of the therapists, but also, when possible, interviews with the patients, as well as with supervisors, colleagues and family members. Celenza describes six findings, the most frequent of which, found in all seventeen cases, was therapist intolerance of the negative transference. Others included unresolved problems with self-esteem; sexualization of pregenital needs; histories of covertly sanctioned boundary transgression by parental figures; unresolved anger toward authority figures; and defensive transformation of countertransference hate into countertransference love. These therapists generally had little insight into their compartmentalized areas of conflict. As a result, she notes, they were "vulnerable to enactments" (p. 381).

Maroda (1998) reports a case involving a young woman who reported to Maroda, in the role of consultant, that she had been in sexual relationships with two previous analytic therapists. The patient had a long-standing pattern of dominating, then discarding, those with whom she had relationships. Maroda concludes the patient's therapists, both women, entered and became hopelessly lost in enactments with her because of their vulnerability to the patient's domination and to each therapist's history of childhood sexual abuse.

A case from my own clinical experience illustrates the ubiquitous role of enactments in sexual misconduct involved a male therapist, who was able to end the work and the relationship before it became fully sexual. The therapist entered an enactment with a seductive, needy, suicidal woman in the context of strains in his own marriage, as his wife became less dependent on him. His enactment occurred in the context of training in a tradition that emphasized doing whatever was necessary to meet the needs of a patient, even if above and beyond the call of duty, and in which training analysts and candidates often socialized in group settings. The analyst's own childhood also included parental sanctioning of his risk-taking as a child and an expectation from an absent father that he would look after his explosive, unpredictable and seductive mother in the father's absence.

CONCLUSIONS REGARDING SEXUAL MISCONDUCT

The work of Gabbard, Gartrell et al., Celenza, and others suggests we must look beyond the notion of analytic conscience to understand the origin of most therapist sexual misconduct. Most of these therapists became lost in the work because of significant compartmentalized characterologic conflicts that left them vulnerable to entering undetected and unanalyzed enactments with their patients. Lost in the dyad, their analytic conscience became permeable to the embodiment of their desire in a way that was justified by what Gabbard has called "lovesickness." What these therapists appear to have lost in the intersubjective intersection of two human lives in the consulting room was not an analytic conscience, but their ability to maintain a transdyadic perspective on the therapeutic work, and their ability to feel their connection to the field's standards and ethical principles.

Our hypothetical trainee would benefit from learning about the connection between enactment and sexual misconduct, as surely as he or she would benefit from instruction in and joining of the field's ethical standards. Our trainees ought to learn that enactments are inevitable and potentially useful therapeutic phenomena, but that they place therapists at risk for sexual misconduct and other boundary violations if not detected, not analyzed from a transdyadic perspective in a state of forbearance, and if new learning from the analysis of the enactment is not utilized in the treatment.

Therapists who engage in sexual misconduct are often not different from us because of a defect in analytic conscience. They are, like the rest of us, fallible human beings, but they have become hopelessly lost in enactments as they struggle to do difficult work with challenging patients whose suffering is real and whose lives are in turmoil.

REFERENCES

Andreasen, N. D. (1997). Linking mind and brain in the study of mental illness: a project for a scientific psychopathology. *Science, 275,* 1586–93.

Baxter, L. R., Schwartz, J. M., and Bergman, K. S. (1992). Caudate glucose metabolic rate changes with both drug and behavior therapy for obsessive-compulsive disorder. *Archives of General Psychiatry, 49,* 618–89.

Belnap, B. A., Iscan, C., and Plakun, E. M. (2004). Residential treatment of personality disorders: The containing function. In J. J. Magnavita, ed., *Handbook of Personality Disorders: Theory and Practice* (pp. 379-97). Hoboken, NJ: John Wiley & Sons.

Bremner, J. D., Randall, P., and Vermetten, E. (1997). Magnetic resonance imaging based measurement of hippocampal volume in posttraumatic stress disorder related to childhood physical and sexual abuse. A preliminary report. *Biological Psychiatry, 41,* 23–32.

Boyer, L. B. (1979). Countertransference with severely regressed patients. In L. Epstein and A. H. Feiner, eds., *Countertransference* (pp. 347-74). New York: Jason Aronson.

Celenza, A. (1998). Precursors to therapist sexual misconduct: preliminary findings. *Psychoanalytic Psychology, 15,* 378–95.

Chused, J. (1997). Discussion of "Observing-participation, mutual enactment, and the new classical models," by I. Hirsch, *Contemporary Psychoanalysis, 33,* 263–77.

Freud, S. (1958). Remembering, repeating and working-through. In J. Strachey, ed. and trans., *The Standard Edition of the Complete Psychological Works of Sigmund Freud,* Vol. 12 (pp. 145–56). London: Hogarth Press. (Original work published 1914)

Fromm, M. G. (1995), What does "borderline" mean? *Psychoanalytic Psychology, 12,* 233–45.

Gabbard, G. O. (1994). Psychotherapists who transgress sexual boundaries with patients. *Bulletin of the Menninger Clinic, 58,* 124–35.

———. (2000). A neurobiologically informed perspective on psychotherapy. *British Journal of Psychiatry,* 177, 117–22.

———. (2003). Miscarriages of psychoanalytic treatment with suicidal patients. *International Journal of Psychoanalysis,* 84, 249–61.

———. (2005). Mind, brain and personality disorders. *American Journal of Psychiatry,* 162, 648–55.

Gartrell, N., Herman, J., and Olarte, S. (1986). Psychiatrist-patient sexual contact: Results of a national survey, I: prevalence. *American Journal of Psychiatry,* 143, 1126–31.

Heimann, P. (1950). On countertransference. *International Journal of Psychoanalysis,* 31, 81–84.

Jacobs, T. J. (1986). On countertransference enactments. *Journal of the American Psychoanalytic Association,* 34, 289–307.

———. (2001). On unconscious communications and covert enactments: Some reflections on their role in the analytic situation. *Psychoanalytic Inquiry,* 21, 4–23.

Joffe, R., Segal, Z., and Singer, W. (1996). Change in thyroid hormone levels following response to cognitive therapy for major depression. *American Journal of Psychiatry,* 153, 411–13.

Johan, M. (1992). Report of the panel on enactments in psychoanalysis. *Journal of the American Psychoanalytic Association,* 40, 827–41.

Maroda, K. J. (1998). Enactment: When the patient's and analyst's pasts converge. *Psychoanalytic Psychology,* 15, 517–35.

McLaughlin, J. (1991). Clinical and theoretical aspects of enactment. *Journal of the American Psychoanalytic Association,* 39, 595–614.

Plakun, E. M. (1998). Enactment and the treatment of abuse survivors. *Harvard Review of Psychiatry,* 5, 318–25.

———. (1999). Sexual misconduct and enactment. *Journal of Psychotherapy Practice and Research,* 8, 284–91.

———. (2001). Making the alliance and taking the transference in work with self-destructive borderline patients. *Journal of Psychotherapy Practice and Research,* 10(4), 269–76.

Putnam, F. W. and Trickett, P. K. (1997). Psychobiological effects of sexual abuse: a longitudinal study. In R. Yehuda and A. C. McFarland, eds., *Psychobiology of Posttraumatic Stress Disorder* (pp. 176–93). New York: New York Academy of Sciences.

Racker, H. (1968). *Transference and Countertransference.* London: Hogarth Press.

Renik, O. (1993). Countertransference enactment and the psychoanalytic process. In M. J. Horowitz, O. F. Kernberg, and E. M. Weinshel, eds., *Psychic Structure an Psychic Change: Essays in Honor of Robert S. Wallerstein* (pp. 135–38). Madison, CT: International Universities Press.

Sandler, J. (1976). Countertransference and role-responsiveness. *International Review of Psychoanalysis,* 3, 43–47.

Shapiro, E. R. and Carr, A. W. (1991). *Lost in Familiar Places.* New Haven, CT: Yale University Press.

Spiegel, D., Bloom, J., and Kraemer, H. D. (1989). Effect of psychosocial treatment on survival of patients with metastatic breast cancer. *Lancet,* ii, 888–91.

Thase, M. E., Fasiczka, A. L., and Berman, S. R. (1998). Electroencephalographic sleep profiles before and after cognitive behavior therapy of depression. *Archives of General Psychiatry,* 55, 138–44.

Wasserman, M. D. (1999). The impact of psychoanalytic theory and a two-person psychology on the empathizing analyst. *International Journal of Psychoanalysis,* 80, 449–64.

Name Index

Subject Index

Contributors

Donna M. Elmendorf, Ph.D., is a psychotherapist and director of the Therapeutic Community Program at the Austen Riggs Center in Stockbridge, MA.

Roger Frie, Ph.D., Psy.D., is assistant clinical professor of medical psychology, Columbia University College of Physicians and Surgeons. He is a graduate of the William Alanson White Institute, and author/editor of three books, including *Understanding Experience, Psychotherapy and Postmodernism* (Routledge, 2003).

M. Gerard Fromm, Ph.D., is the Evelyn Stefansson Nef Director of the Erikson Institute for Education and Research of the Austen Riggs Center. He is a faculty member of the Massachusetts Institute for Psychoanalysis and guest faculty of the Berkshire Psychoanalytic Institute. He is also the current president of the Center for the Study of Groups and Social Systems. Fromm has written on a number of psychoanalytic subjects and edited, with Bruce L. Smith, Ph.D., *The Facilitating Environment: Clinical Applications of Winnicott's Theory.*

Lila J. Kalinich, M.D., is a training and supervising analyst at the Columbia Psychoanalytic Center for Training and Research, and an associate clinical professor of psychiatry at Columbia University. She is also the president of the Association for Psychoanalytic Medicine in New York City. Dr. Kalinich has written in several interdisciplinary areas including cultural, political and religious studies. She also teaches a course on Freud to undergraduate students at Columbia College.

Arnold Modell, M.D., is a training and supervising analyst at the Boston Psychoanalytic Institute and a clinical professor of psychiatry at the Harvard Medical School. His most recent books include *The Private Self* (Harvard University Press) and *Imagination and the Meaningful Brain* (MIT Press).

John P. Muller, Ph.D., is a clinical psychologist and psychoanalyst and director of training at the Austen Riggs Center, Stockbridge, MA. He has published widely on semiotics and psychoanalysis.

Eric M. Plakun, M.D., is the director of Admissions at the Austen Riggs Center in Stockbridge, MA where he is also a treatment team leader, psychotherapy supervisor, and co-principal investigator of a prospective follow-along study of treatment outcome. Dr. Plakun is also a clinical instructor of psychiatry at the Harvard Medical School.

Richard B. Simpson, M.D., is a psychoanalyst in private practice in Toronto. He is a member of La Société Psychanalytique de Montréal and the Lacanian Clinical Forum. French psychoanalysis in all its forms is his major area of interest and he has published articles in the *Psychoanalytic Quarterly* introducing key aspects of French psychoanalysis.

Jane G. Tillman, Ph.D., is a clinical psychologist, supervisor, treatment team leader, and the chair of External Education at the Austen Riggs Center in Stockbridge, MA.